Reliability Centered Maintenance using...

RCM Blitz

By Douglas Plucknette

Reliability Centered Maintenance using...

RCM Blitz™

2nd Edition

Douglas J. Plucknette

ISBN 978-0-9838741-6-4
HF032017

© 2013-2016 NetexpressUSA dba Reliabilityweb.com
(Reliabilityweb.com)
Printed in the United States of America.
All rights reserved.

This book, or any parts thereof may not be reproduced, stored in a retrieval system, or transmitted in any form without the permission of the publisher.

Opinions expressed in this book are solely the author's and do not necessarily reflect the views of the Publisher.

Publisher: Reliabilityweb.com
Cover Design: Nicola Behr
Layout and Design: Sara Soto

For information: Reliabilityweb.com
www.reliabilityweb.com
8991 Daniels Center Drive, Suite 105
Fort Myers, FL 33912
Toll Free: 888-575-1245, Phone: 239-333-2500
Email: crm@reliabilityweb.com

10 9 8 7 6 5 4 3

Table of Contents

Dedication		v
Acknowledgement		viii
1	**Introduction**	1
2	**Up-Front Tasks**	11
	Document Reliability Measures	13
	Operational History Report	19
	Gathering Necessary Information	23
	Estimating RCM Analysis Size	25
	Selecting and Training Your RCM Team	32
	The RCM Analysis Contract	35
	Train Your RCM Team	39
3	**Probability and Consequence**	41
4	**Functions and Functional Failures**	47
	Main or System Functions	47
	Support Functions	50
	Functional Failures	55
5	**FMECA**	61
	Failure Modes and Probability of Failure	61
	Failure Effects and Consequences	70
	RCM Decision Process	78
	Selecting Maintenance Tasks	85
	Spare Parts	108
6	**Follow-Up Tasks**	111
	Completing Your RCM Analysis	111
	Proofreading Your RCM Analysis	114
	Prioritization and RCM Implementation	115
	The RCM Analysis Report	119
	RCM Review Meeting	120
	Tracking Results	123
7	**General RCM Topics**	127
8	**Scoring Your RCM Effort**	147
	Closing	155
	About the Author	158

Dedication

In the time it took to write this book, I was reminded of the countless people I have lived and worked with. Without our time spent together, and the life experiences we shared, I would never have gained the knowledge necessary to develop the RCM Blitz™ method; which in turn led me to instruct, and facilitate, Reliability Centered Maintenance in companies around the world.

First and foremost, I would like to thank my wife of twenty-six years, and partner for life, Leslie Plucknette. It was your love and faith in me that provided the inspiration and courage to leave Eastman Kodak and create Reliability Solutions, Inc. I will never forget the many nights we spent together in our hot tub weighing the pros and cons of what turned out to be a life- changing decision for both of us. After nearly ten years of hectic travel, our love remains stronger than ever and each night that I'm away and we talk on the phone, I miss you more and can't wait to be home in your arms.

To our children, Katie, Jared and Emily, words cannot describe how proud I am of each of you and what you have accomplished in your short lives. I cherish the time we have spent together as a family and look forward to what your futures will bring. To any parents who have to keep three balls in the air and still make concerts, sporting events and proms, you can understand the difficulty in traveling for a living and being there as well. I'm proud to say I've missed less than you can count on one hand, but those I did miss were some of the most painful nights of my life. Thank you for your kindness and understanding. I will love you forever.

To my mom and dad, Tom and Joyce Plucknette, thank you for being a living example of what marriage is supposed to be and for being there when I could not. Over the years those who have had to suffer through RCM Blitz™ training and anyone who has read my articles in Uptime magazine, knows the impact my dad has had on my career. He taught us what brains, hard work and ethics are all about.

To my family friend and attorney, John Considine, and brother, Tom Plucknette Jr., the two people I leaned on and trusted when I needed the knowledge and experience necessary to start Reliability Solutions.

To my friends and colleagues from Eastman Kodak, while we worked for a shrinking giant that suffered from poor executive leadership, those of us who worked in the field of maintenance and reliability continued to strive for ingenuity and excellence. I have always been proud to say I worked for a company who understood the value of training, continuing education, and world class maintenance. I have a huge list of Kodak people who helped to mold my career, starting off with Jerry Hagerty, one of the founders of SMRP and the brainchild of Kodak's world-wide reliability organization GERE, and Maurice (Maury) Torrey who got stuck having me as a RCM mentor and with whom I worked to create RCM Blitz™. To the crew from Polymer, where I started my Kodak career as a pipefitter, the world deserves to know that the best maintenance crew ever assembled worked Polymer building 317, Mark Zimmerman, Kevin Skelly, Bob McGonigal, Gary Sutphen, Chris (Harve Duty) Harvey, Gene Falco, Barry Lotz, Dave (Big Bird) Shuler, Tom Avrey, John Palmer, Andy Liszkay and Press (The Fatman) Wilcox. I wish I could duplicate the synergy, knowledge, and work ethic of this crew and sell it. Together we turned the department where no-one wanted to work into the place no-one wanted to leave.

To the people at Whirlpool Findlay, Ohio, my first customers, and thank God, my first success story. Without the hard work, drive and determination of Kirk Wolfinger, Tom Meyer, John (Richard) Word and Jim Drey, RCM Blitz™ would have been the program of the month. It is no coincidence that Whirlpool Findlay is a world-class company. This plant has all the requirements: Leadership, Structure, Discipline and people from top to bottom who live and breathe continuous improvement.

I owe a huge thank you to the Reliability Leaders of Cargill. Prior to 2002, I had no idea the largest privately held company in the world even existed, but I am thankful for the day some of their best sat in on the Whirlpool SMRP presentation! What started as a pilot RCM Blitz™ analysis at Cargill nearly six years ago, is now the preferred methodology and Select Supplier of Reliability Centered Maintenance, thanks to the support and belief of the following people: Terry Harris (Now of Reliable Process Solutions), Rick Baldridge, Oilseeds Reliability Leader, and Tim Goshert, World-Wide Reliability Leader. These guys know reliability and leadership better than anyone in the business. Companies around the world would be smart to model Cargill's Reliability Center of Excellence. I have worked at Cargill facilities around the world and it would be wrong not to mention some of the people who believe in, and sponsor the RCM Blitz™ process: Paul de

Ruijter and Walter Nijsen - Cargill Europe, Chris Hein - Memphis, Craig Yeager - Salt Reliability Leader, Steve Mikolajcik and Greg Wegner - Meat Solutions, Cody Steinmetz - Sidney Ohio, Jason Hartman - Wilbur Chocolate, and last but not least, Derek Burley - Blair, Nebraska.

To my largest effort to date, Invista, I can still remember the day I met with Keith Carlin and Bart Lee and they informed me they wanted to train nearly 200 RCM facilitators at 40 sites in countries around the world in six different languages in the next 8 to 12 months. And I told them I could do it, GULP! Thank you for your continued faith in the process. I am excited by the continuing progress and results. Next up RCM in China!

Thank you once again to some of the legends of reliability whom I consider friends and mentors, Jack Nicholas Jr., Ron Moore, and Mark Galley. I someday hope to draw the audience, respect, and recognition you have each earned through your tireless dedication in educating the rest of us about reliability.

In July of 2007, my long-term goal of making RCM Blitz™ the preferred RCM methodology around the world came a huge step closer when John Schultz and John Langhorne of Allied Reliability Group made the decision to purchase exclusive license to RCM Blitz™. Having known these two through my relationship with Cargill for years, they were the only two people in the world I would have trusted to build a network that could deliver this process to the masses. Through this relationship, I have been afforded the time and peace of mind to write this book and for that I am grateful. No company in the world has the experience, knowledge and people to deliver the key elements of reliability like those at Allied Reliability Group.

Finally, thanks to the person responsible for saving RCM Blitz™, Reliability Web's, Terry O'Hanlon. In September of 2001, I had just completed eight months of training and mentoring RCM facilitators at Coors Brewing, then came September 11th, and almost immediately after, the Enron scandal. Reliability Solutions, Inc. closed out 2001 well in the black and then along came 2002. From January 2002 to August 2002, while dumping thousands of dollars into poorly placed ads and marketing, I booked a stellar two weeks of work! In June 2002, by chance, I found the newly formed ReliabilityWeb website on-line and not long after I began having regular phone conversations with Terry. Being the master of marketing and reliability that he is, I soon had my first very affordable I-Presentation up and running on ReliabilityWeb and within the first week I had well over 1000 leads, real names, addresses and phone numbers of people who were interested in RCM Blitz™! From that day forward I knew I had found a person and a place where I could keep the RCM Blitz™ name in front of the masses. From that time forward I have worked with Terry to create information and content for ReliabilityWeb, along with presentations at each year's RCM and IMC conference. For years I have been proud to call Terry O'Hanlon and all the people at ReliabilityWeb, friends. Thanks Terry!

Acknowledgement

Reliabilityweb.com would like to thank Allied Reliability for the use of figures, graphs and charts throughout this document.

www.alliedreliability.com

CHAPTER 1
Introduction

I have spent time over the last fifteen years working with customers around the world to facilitate Reliability Centered Maintenance analyses on their critical assets. I have visited hundreds of plants and met with thousands of people. In doing so, I have often been asked, "Have you written a book on RCM Blitz™?" In my opinion, the last thing the world needed was another book about Reliability Centered Maintenance. I have continued to recommend the original RCM document written by Stan Nowlan and Howard Heap as well as other articles, white papers, and books written by myself and other practitioners of RCM.

In nearly every week-long facilitator course I instruct, I inform the class that I'm not the smartest person in the world. I'm the type of person that has to read information more than once to truly understand what I'm trying to learn. If I'm trying to learn something new, I have to try the task several times before I perform it to my satisfaction, and most importantly, I'm not afraid to learn from my mistakes. If I really want to learn something, I watch someone else do it, I pay close attention to detail, and ask the person questions on specific steps for clarification. I then record each step in my mind, or on paper, and work to memorize the process and move forward. The step-by-step procedure to learn, and then perfect, works for me and this is why I love RCM. Learn the steps, follow the steps, apply the steps, stick to the process and success is easy. Like I said, I'm not the smartest person in the world.

I learned the RCM process the way most people do. I signed up for a training class, attended the course and took piles of notes. My first analysis was ugly, overdone, detailed to a level beyond reality. It took three months to complete and ended up in a notebook on the top shelf of my desk nestled tightly between two other programs of the month. My first attempt at a proven process was a failure. The notebook and its contents stared back at me like a closing relief pitcher who just hurled his first pitch past me in the bottom of the ninth!

I told myself, "dig in, relax, and take a breath", hitting is a process that only succeeds when one swings the bat. Go back to the process and follow the proven steps.

Going back, for me, meant to the original process that Nowlan and Heap developed. Since they completed the report on Reliability Centered Maintenance, people have been adopting the process and then adding to it, or worse, taking steps away to make the process faster.

I tore into the 466 pages of government detail and terms, taking notes on each step and reviewing how they applied each step in the case study. What I found in reading the document is that most people took a simple process and made it more complex. I also came away with a much better understanding of how RCM is supposed to work.

In my mind, Reliability Centered Maintenance is very similar to Root Cause Analysis. RCM is all about the relationship between Cause and Effect. Through the identification of causes, or failure modes, we can look to mitigate each failure by taking a pro-active approach to maintenance. Looking back on my first completed RCM analysis, it was clear where I had made several mistakes. In re-writing the failure modes from that analysis and applying them to the Nowlan and Heap process and decision diagram, the resulting tasks now made sense.

At this time I made the decision to sit down at the drawing board to develop a RCM Methodology that was simple and focused on manufacturing reliability. I would stick to a 7-step process and develop a decision diagram that made clear, "No Scheduled Maintenance", was not the end of the RCM decision process.

My second RCM analysis was on a process that filled cubes of photo chemicals. As this system was suffering overall equipment effectiveness (OEE) of 46%, this same process was in the approval stages for a healthy capital up-grade. In selecting this process, I had studied the production data for several months, noticing some drastic changes in shiftly, daily, and weekly thru-put as well as downtime. In talking about the asset with operations and maintenance personnel prior to the RCM analysis, I learned our largest causes of downtime stemmed around equipment set-up and product change-over. Any time we changed cube size, it took hours to make the change and several hours to make the machine run consistently. I understood now that part of the main function of this asset would include being able to change product types and sizes.

In taking time to understand the functionality of this asset, and each of the components or support functions, I now had a clear road map to make this RCM a successful effort. With this information, and several months of OEE (Overall Equipment Effectiveness) data that showed where our key manufacturing losses were located, I was now confident this RCM would deliver results in improved reliability for a critical asset.

In taking the time to learn about this asset, I was able to meet the key operators and maintenance people who were considered experts on this machine and when I scheduled the week-long RCM analysis I made sure that these people were part of the RCM team.

Over the next three months, the second RCM was completed and eighty-five percent of the mitigating tasks were implemented, scheduled and performed. Maintenance and Operations personnel were trained to perform each task, including product changes as well as PM inspections. In the fourth month following the RCM analysis, the asset OEE was consistently above 82%. The total cost to perform the RCM analysis and implement the tasks was less than $30,000 and in the sixth month following the RCM, the capital upgrade project to replace the line was scrapped.

In the second RCM analysis, I took the time to write down several key learning's that I share today as part of the RCM Blitz™ Facilitator training program:

1. RCM works best on critical assets.

2. Take time up front to measure OEE - Identify/Locate key manufacturing losses.

3. Taking too long to complete a RCM is a waste of time and only results in people losing patience and focus. Complete the RCM in one week by scheduling your team to meet all day for 5 days.

4. Use the main and support functions to create a clear roadmap for your RCM analysis.

5. Begin to complete the RCM tasks as soon as the RCM is complete and set aggressive due dates to complete them.

6. Keep the RCM team and local managers up to date on the progress of implementation. Keeping them informed keeps them engaged and excited about the process.

7. Continue to track and report OEE following the RCM analysis and task implementation. This is the best way to clearly show the impact of a complete maintenance strategy on critical assets.

Following the success of this second RCM analysis, I now had the attention of our plant manager, the maintenance manager, and more importantly, the attention of our world-wide reliability manager. Having a grand total of one successful RCM analysis as part of my resume, Maurice Torrey and I made the decision to quickly develop a traditional, fast, and effective RCM methodology, database, and training program. Working together over the next four weeks, the Kodak Blitz RCM process was developed from my notes and the work of Stanley Nowlan and Howard Heap. Following our presentation to Global Equipment Reliability Engineering (GERE) manager, Diane Newhouse and Jerome (Jerry) Haggerty, GERE Training Manager, we were given two months to select a pilot asset, train a team, perform the RCM analysis and implement the tasks. In this short envelope, we were also charged with submitting all of our RCM training materials to corporate attorneys to acquire copyrights, and at the same time ensure there were no copyright or trademark violations. This would prove to be a valuable learning experience for yours truly!

Over the next three months, Maury and I, completed two more successful analyses, developed a RCM participant and facilitator training module and created a simple Access database to help track and report each RCM analysis. In November of 1997, we were hired into Kodak's GERE organization as the world-wide trainers and mentors for Blitz RCM.

Over the next 18 months we performed RCM analyses, provided RCM facilitator training and mentoring around the world and tracked the progress, implementation and success of Blitz RCM for the company. It was during this time that I discovered, for the second time in my life, that I enjoyed what I did for a living, but it was the first time in my life that I felt that I was good at what I did. My life at the time was very busy. I had a wife, three children, worked a full-time job at Kodak, attended night school for Reliability Engineering at RIT, tended bar part-time at the Rochester Auditorium Theatre and coached Little League baseball in the summer. While I was busy, life was indeed good!

In October of 1999, Maury and I were asked to present a paper on Blitz RCM at the SMRP national conference in Denver, Colorado. Following the conference presentation, life as I enjoyed it quickly began to change; the success of RCM at Kodak had drawn the attention of Kodak managers. Maury and I began to interview for various positions within the company. I was also receiving calls outside Kodak from companies/managers who had attended the SMRP conference. Each company that made contact had tried and failed at RCM, several were interested in learning more about Blitz RCM, and a few made direct job offers looking for someone to manage RCM. While the offers were substantially more than I was ever paid at Kodak, moving my family was not an option!

With change coming fast, I needed to quickly make a good decision. Being a slow learner, I needed to make sure it was the right one. I turned to a proven process, the writings of Dale Carnegie, and the experience/wisdom/advice of some close friends. I spent November of 1999, building the business plan for Reliability Solutions, Incorporated under the advice of my brother Tom Plucknette, president of MTR (Machine Tool Research) and attorney, John Considine. I spent nearly an hour every night that month in the hot-tub with my wife, Leslie, reviewing the business plan and the potential risks associated with leaving a shrinking giant like Eastman Kodak. With nineteen years of experience at Kodak, and 12-credit hours short of a Bachelor's Degree, I was close to making the decision. I went to Maury and offered to have him join me. Being much closer to the benefits of retirement, Maury elected to stay on at Kodak, I, in turn, had a decision to make.

Following the Thanksgiving holidays, I made two phone calls. The first was to Tom Meyer of Whirlpool, the second was to Jim Borowski of National Steel. I offered to provide them with RCM Facilitator Training and mentoring services as a consultant. Each agreed to allow me to come in and present a detailed plan to company management. Following consecutive trips to Detroit, Michigan and Findlay, Ohio, I came home with two signed contracts in hand. The difficult decision was now made easy; the two contracts totaled three times my annual Kodak salary. I could leave the company, perform the work, fall flat on my face and still have two and a half years to finish college and find a better job. I was excited to deliver my two-week notice, and start a company where pay for performance was a reality, and not a phrase.

On December 15, 1999, I informed Eastman Kodak that I would be leaving to start Reliability Solutions. In thanks for what I had learned in gaining copyright for Kodak, I granted the company permission to continue to use a process I had developed as an hourly employee, but was never compensated for. Two weeks later, I left the company with a whopping $23,000 in annuity and my 401K. Nearly everyone I talked to at Kodak thought I was crazy. I wasn't crazy! I had a company, a proven product, two contracts and a wife who supported my confidence. I was free!

RCM Blitz™

Looking back through my notes over the past fifteen years, I can point to several things that made RCM Blitz™ and Reliability Solutions, Inc. a success. First and most important, was the success that the Whirlpool dishwasher plant in Findlay, Ohio had with the process. I got lucky in the that the Whirlpool RCM team included a driven Maintenance and Engineering Manager in Kirk Wolfinger, a motivated RCM Facilitator in Richard Word, and experience in co-facilitators Tom Meyer and Jim Drey. The Whirlpool RCM team performed and implemented 37 RCM analyses in less than three years, and even better, they were not afraid to share with anyone interested how they succeeded, delivering presentations at SMRP, and agreeing to an article on the effort in MRO Today.

The following are notes I have made over the last several years regarding why Reliability Solutions Inc. was a success, and more important, why RCM Blitz™ works.

RCM Blitz™ Success Factors

1. Work with an open mind, your success depends on the success of your clients.

2. Build a relationship with clients by becoming engaged in how they plan to perform and implement RCM. Build a plan with each company. Do your best to make them succeed.

3. Turn people on to RCM by sharing success, showing models of successful efforts, and actual analysis results, when applicable.

4. Accept the fact that RCM is boring and takes a high level of patience, then work hard as a facilitator or instructor to make the process fun, engaging and entertaining.

5. Develop a process to train and certify facilitators. Follow the process and don't ever shortcut that process to make people happy. Certified RCM Blitz™ Facilitators will perform at a level above others because they have worked to achieve certification.

6. Always listen to your customers and facilitators when it comes to the RCM Blitz™ process. Some of the best process improvements have come from practitioners who have asked to try a simple change, or add a field to the database. Process improvement is dependent on having an open mind.

7. Confront RCM Failures with the same level of detail you use to discover failure modes. Each RCM failure may have one, or more, causes. In working to identify and mitigate these causes, you will be working to ensure the success of your customers.

8. Always, Always, Always, follow the RCM Blitz™ process flow. Remember, it is your job as a certified facilitator to follow the process and ask the questions. Successful RCM comes only from facilitators who follow the process and allow the experts on the RCM team to provide the answers.

While I believed for a long time the world did not need another book on RCM, after nine years of facilitating analyses, as well as training and mentoring RCM Blitz™ facilitators, I have decided, with the constant prodding of customers and friends, the world does need one good book on RCM Blitz™!

In closing, I would like to share a conversation I had with my son, Jared, back in the summer of 2002. Jared was about to become a freshman in high school and I had been performing RCM analysis on an off-shore oil platform in California.

Leaning against the edge of the pool we had the following conversation:

Jared: "Dad, just what does your company do for other companies?"

Doug: "We facilitate a process that helps companies develop a maintenance strategy to make sure their equipment runs safe and reliable."

Jared: "But how do you know about all that equipment? You showed me the pictures you took of the oil platform from the helicopter, how do you know about oil platforms?"

Doug: "I don't know anything about oil platforms. I know about my process. I bring in a team of people from the oil company who are experts on the equipment and ask them questions about their equipment. Then when we finish we send a report on the recommendations."

Jared: "So, their people know what needs to be done? You just ask the questions and record the information?"

Doug: "Yep, that's it!"

Jared: "Dad, how long do you expect this to last?"

Our conversation inspired RCM Success Factor #8:

Always follow the process and let the experts provide the answers. Become an expert in Reliability Centered Maintenance and your customers will have success using the process. Make a growing list of successful customers and RCM Blitz™ will be known around the world.

RCM Blitz™ Process Flow

The standard for traditional methods of Reliability Centered Maintenance can be found in SAE standard JA1011. This standard can be simplified by following closely the seven steps of RCM.

While the RCM Blitz™ methodology meets the standards of both, I offer the following process flow diagram to my facilitators in training.

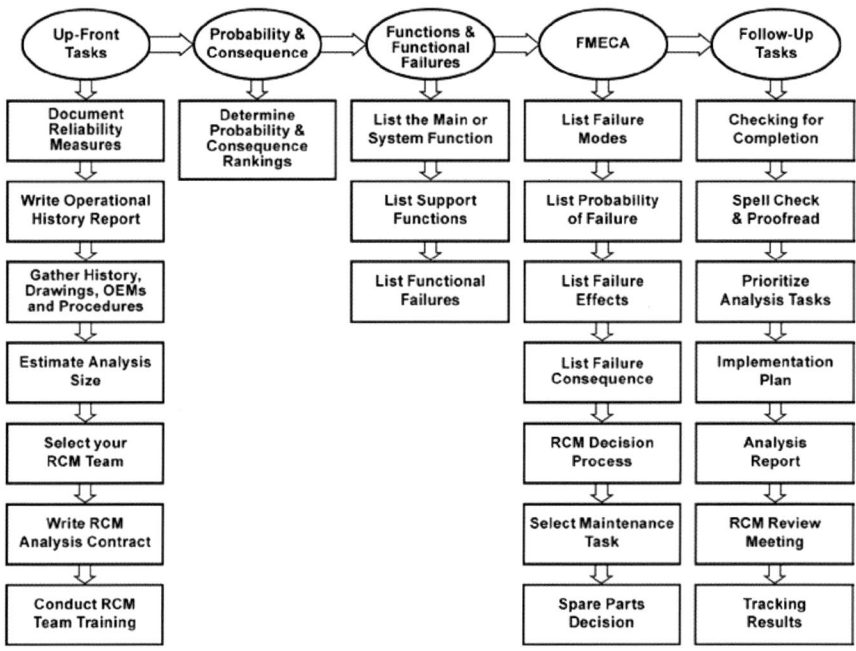

Looking at the RCM Blitz™ process, we start with Up-Front tasks. The steps within the process guide the facilitator to select qualified assets for analysis, and prepare the facilitators and team for success. Up-Front tasks must be completed prior to scheduling and performing the RCM analysis. I have never seen a RCM team fail when all of the Up-Front tasks have been completed. I have seen several teams fail when one, or more, of these steps are not completed.

The 5 Major Steps of RCM Blitz™

1. **Up-Front Tasks -** Set the RCM Facilitators and Team up for success.

2. **Probability and Consequence -** Building the groundwork for understanding the importance of each individual failure mode and developing sound methods to prioritize RCM tasks.

3. **Functions and Functional Failures -** The roadmap to successful RCM analysis. World class companies understand the importance of addressing maintenance at the functional failure level.

4. **FMECA** - The heart and soul of Reliability Centered Maintenance, this is where the work gets done, identifying failure modes, describing failure effects and developing tasks.

5. **Follow-Up Tasks** - Designed to help the team quickly move forward and drive the implementation of the RCM tasks. While Implementation may be known as the graveyard of RCM, I tell my facilitators that every failed RCM analysis has a gravedigger, and if you see someone with a shovel, take it away. Follow-up is just as important as the analysis itself and like everything else it has a process.

This book will be laid out in chapters that deal with working through the 5 major steps of the RCM Blitz™ process flow model. While I recognize that five steps may seem incomplete when it comes to RCM, it is important to understand that each major step may contain several individual steps that are critical in completing a thorough RCM analysis.

CHAPTER 2
Up - Front Tasks

Selecting Assets For RCM Analysis

I like to call Reliability Centered Maintenance a "reliability tool". The reason I like the phrase "reliability tool", is that the word tool implies, like other tools, that RCM was designed for a specific use. Like other tools, if we try to use RCM for the wrong application, we may not end up with a positive result.

When I got into the business of facilitating RCM fifteen years ago, it was commonplace to hear that, "RCM should be applied to every asset your company owns. The business case for RCM is driven by safety performance and if you don't apply RCM to all your assets, bad things will happen and people will die." This concept of how we should apply Reliability Centered Maintenance came from its use in the airline industry, and in that application it makes sense. Think about it, on an airliner, the failure of even some of the smallest and seemingly insignificant devices could result in a fire, ending with catastrophic results. Worse than the thought of applying RCM to every single asset, were the consequences of challenging this belief.

In 1999, I presented a paper on RCM at the SMRP Annual Conference in Denver, Colorado. At this conference, we discussed how we applied RCM Blitz™ (then known as Blitz RCM) to our critical assets, as this was where we experienced the most success regarding return on investment. Well, from the reaction of other RCM consultants in the room, you would have thought we just told the conference attendees the world was flat!

- "You can't just apply RCM to critical assets, this is dangerous."
- "What you are doing goes completely against what other experts are saying."
- "Safety, not cost benefit, should be the driving force behind why a company needs RCM to set a complete maintenance strategy."

Anyone who has ever attended a SMRP or RCM conference has heard the above arguments when it comes to RCM. Each of these points is valid to a certain extent, they just aren't the only reasons why a company should work to create a RCM culture. Consider the following list of potential benefits provided by a thorough RCM Blitz™ analysis:

- Improved Equipment Reliability (OEE - Overall Equipment Effectiveness)
- A Reduction in Environmental, Health and Safety Incidents and Accidents
- Reduced Emergency and Demand Maintenance
- Reduced Equipment Down Time
- Reduced Secondary Equipment Damage
- Lower Maintenance Costs
- Improved Process Knowledge and Troubleshooting Skills for Operations and Maintenance Personnel
- Improved Productivity
- Improved Product Quality
- Reduced Unit Cost of Product
- Increased Company/Product Profit Margins

After reading the list, which of the above benefits would work best to help you convince your management and corporate directors to invest in Reliability Centered Maintenance? Suppose you also work for a company who has a world-class health, safety and environmental record. How do you now convince this same team of managers that you need RCM for the sake of safety? The truth is you won't convince this team they need RCM for safety reasons. But now, show this same team some reliability measures for critical assets, compared to your operational, speed, and quality losses, and show them the potential production that could be achieved by performing RCM and eliminating those losses. You now have a winner! Return on investment is the best way to sell RCM in manufacturing, and the additional quality, health, safety, and environmental benefits are icing on the cake.

Up-Front Tasks
Document Reliability Measures

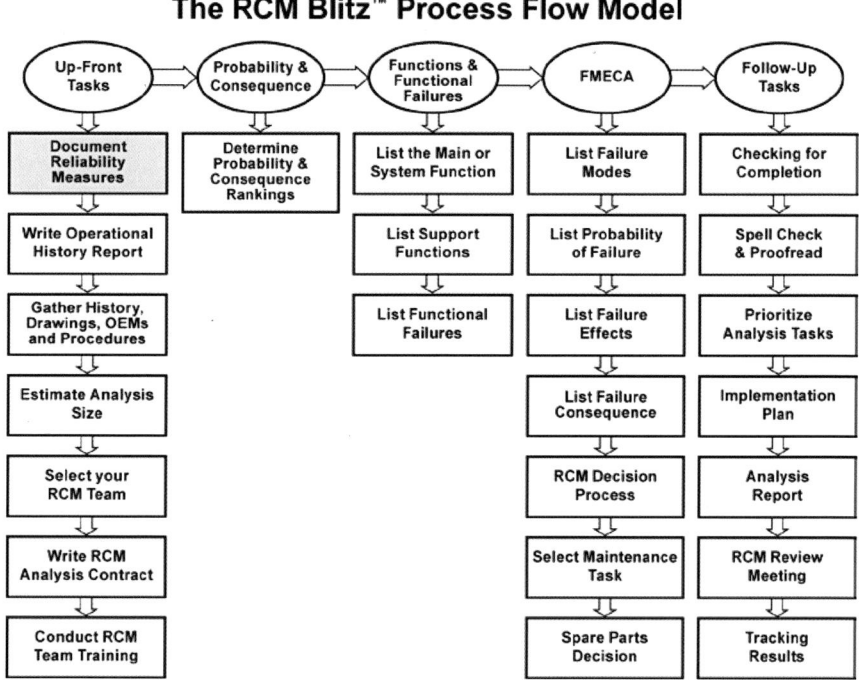

There is always a level of excitement that goes along with the first analysis, as a result, I am most often offered the company's problem child of the week, or month, for this first analysis. I meet this offer with the request for formal data. Reliability Centered Maintenance is all about leadership, structure, and discipline. Show me the process you used to select your first asset for analysis. To make RCM become a part of your company culture, you need to select winners, critical assets that are suffering with equipment-related quality, speed, and operational losses. Follow this formula, perform your RCM analysis, implement the tasks and you will have a huge winner.

To make this clear, you need to start with critical assets. If your company hasn't already done so, you will need to perform an asset criticality assessment. This can be accomplished by hiring a consulting company who has experience in criticality assessment tools, or by developing a criticality assessment tool and working with operations and maintenance to perform the assessment.

Your asset criticality assessment tool should take in the following criteria at a minimum:

- Effect on Health/Safety
- Effect on the Environment
- Effect on Production
- Effect on Quality
- Cost of Repair

Each asset in your plant should now be ranked on how it affects each category (using a 1 through 5 ranking scale). Listed below are the definitions we developed for the 1 to 5 ranking scale for Effect on Health and Safety:

Probability of Asset Failure

1. It is highly improbable that a failure could occur in 1:10,000 years.
2. Failure of this component is not likely in 1:1000 years.
3. This asset has failed before on similar assets but not this machine.
4. This asset has failed before.
5. This is a dominant failure mode.

Consequence of Asset Failure

1. Failure of this asset has no impact on the business.
2. Failure results in total expenses exceeding $1000.
3. Failure expense exceeds $10,000 or First Aid Injury.
4. Failure expense exceeds $25,000 or OSHA Reportable Incident.
5. Failure expense exceeds $100,000 or Loss Time Incident, Dismemberment or Death.

For each asset, you will now "rank and total" probability and consequence, and calculate the sum for each consequence category. Then, total the sum of all the consequence categories, this is your asset rank number, those with the highest rank number are your most critical assets.

Having worked through criticality analysis with two companies, and across varied business units, I would also recommend that if your company has yet to perform asset criticality analysis, the easiest and most cost-effective way is to contract it out. A company like Allied Reliability can perform a criticality analysis on hundreds of assets (in the same amount of time your company will take to develop the first draft of your criteria) at about half the cost.

Now that you have identified your critical assets, you should begin to measure critical asset reliability using OEE (Overall Equipment Effectiveness) and TEEP (Total Effective Equipment Performance) in terms that clearly view good product manufactured and key manufacturing losses. Good Reliability Engineers use OEE/TEEP not only as a Reliability Measure, but as a Reliability Tool, to locate where losses are occurring and what needs to be done to reduce those losses.

Having performed hundreds of RCM Blitz™ analyses, I can safely say that when fully implemented, the RCM Blitz™ process does a fantastic job of reducing and eliminating equipment related - Operational, Speed and Quality losses.

Reliability Measures -

OEE (Overall Equipment Effectiveness) - Measures equipment performance against scheduled time.
TEEP (Total Effective Equipment Performance) - Measures equipment performance against total time.
Value
- Integration of quality, throughput, and efficiency into one common metric.
- The ability to recognize where reliability losses are, and select a reliability tool to reduce those losses.
- Easy to use and can be calculated by shift, daily, weekly or monthly.
- Looks at more than the traditional manufacturing metrics of waste and cycle time.
- Helps teams and work groups create healthy goals and competition.

Reporting Proposal - Report OEE/TEEP Data in Terms of Losses
- Good Product Manufactured (First Pass Yield)
- Operational Losses (Unscheduled Down Time)
- Planned Losses (Scheduled Down Time)
- Speed Losses (Product lost due to running at reduced speed)
- Quality Losses (Product lost due to waste, rework, holds)

Definitions - It is important in using a process reliability measure that everyone using the measure has a common understanding of the terms.

This makes the measure consistent across industries. There is often a temptation to make a measure fit your business because the first number calculated doesn't meet someone's expectations. The intent of these measures is to help you identify where your losses are and then work to reduce those losses. The best way to improve your final numbers is to identify where your losses are and set goals to reduce those losses.

Good Product - This is the amount of time "good product" was produced or the number of "good units" produced. The remainder of time the equipment was not used will result in some type of measured loss. Product manufactured in this time must be good quality product and meet all customer specifications. Measure can be in units or time but must be consistent.

Operational Losses - Time your equipment is not producing product when it was scheduled to be running. This is down time due to: equipment failure, equipment set-up, product change-over, lack of material or labor, utility-supply problems, product jams, computer or PLC related downtime. Measure can be in terms of units or time.

Planned Losses - This is time the factory is not scheduled to run but could run. Time where there is no demand for product. Things included in the planned loss bucket are weekends and holidays, capital improvement time, cleaning time, breaks and lunches, meetings, preventive maintenance.

Quality Losses - Time the factory ran but was making product that did not meet quality or first-pass yield specifications. The time it took to manufacture units that were held for inspection, waste, or re-worked.

Speed Losses - Time lost due to running product at a reduced speed. If the equipment were scheduled to run at 100 units per hour, or 100 feet per hour, and actually ran at slower than expected speeds, this would result in lost time or units. The extra time it took to meet that schedule is a loss.

The categories listed are generic and can be tailored to fit your business model. What is important is that you begin using OEE and TEEP to measure the reliability of your critical assets and in doing so you begin to understand which assets are performing, and more importantly, the critical assets that are not performing. The beauty of measuring OEE and TEEP using this method is that it will clearly show each loss category so that you can begin to pinpoint critical assets that are good candidates for RCM analysis.

RCM has proven effective in reducing equipment related Operational, Speed and Quality losses and can also significantly reduce losses related to equipment start-up, change-over, as well as other human-error related losses. When I worked as a Reliability Engineer and RCM Facilitator, I found great value in breaking each loss category into a Pareto diagram to clearly show the causes responsible for each. In doing so, I could say, with absolute certainty, a RCM analysis would not only improve asset reliability but would also quickly pay for the cost of performing the analysis and implementing the task.

Looking at the steps of the RCM Blitz™ process, the one that gets the most push back is measuring OEE. Looking at today's business world, we measure a number of things on a daily, weekly, monthly and annual basis. I would offer that very few of these measures have the power of OEE. I have personally witnessed companies who began measuring OEE on critical assets prior to starting their RCM effort, clearly posted the OEE each shift on these assets and began to see results without having made one change to their manufacturing process. The measure alone creates a goal to improve and increases communication between shifts, generating questions and conversations. "What happened last night? What did you change? What was broken? How is it running now?" If it were up to me, every company starting an effort in reliability would start with measuring OEE. OEE produces the information necessary to generate a goal, and the path to reach that goal.

The greatest value in performing criticality analysis, and tracking reliability measures on your critical assets, comes following the implementation of your RCM tasks. As the reliability of these assets increases beyond most people's expectations, you can clearly show the value of RCM, as reliable assets make all other aspects of the manufacturing business easier. For those who have never experienced this, reliability makes all of the following more efficient and easier to perform:

- Production Scheduling
- Staff Scheduling
- The Manufacturing of Quality Products
- Maintenance Planning and Scheduling
- On-Time Delivery of Products

Additionally, companies who understand reliability, and have reliable assets, have less Health, Safety and Environmental incidents and accidents, decreased maintenance costs as well as decreased costs to manufacture products. As a result, the unit cost of your product is also reduced, increasing profits, giving your company a competitive advantage in the marketplace!

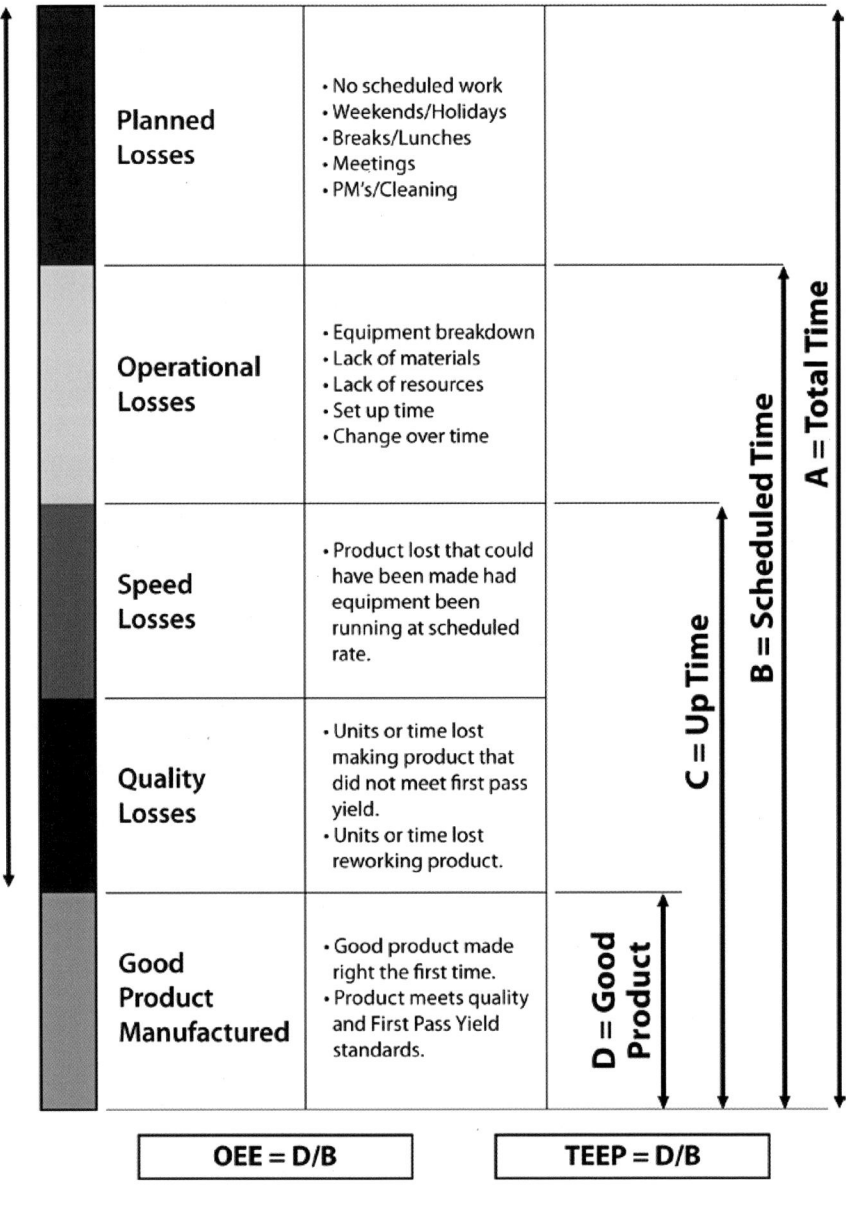

Up - Front Tasks
Writing an Operational History Report

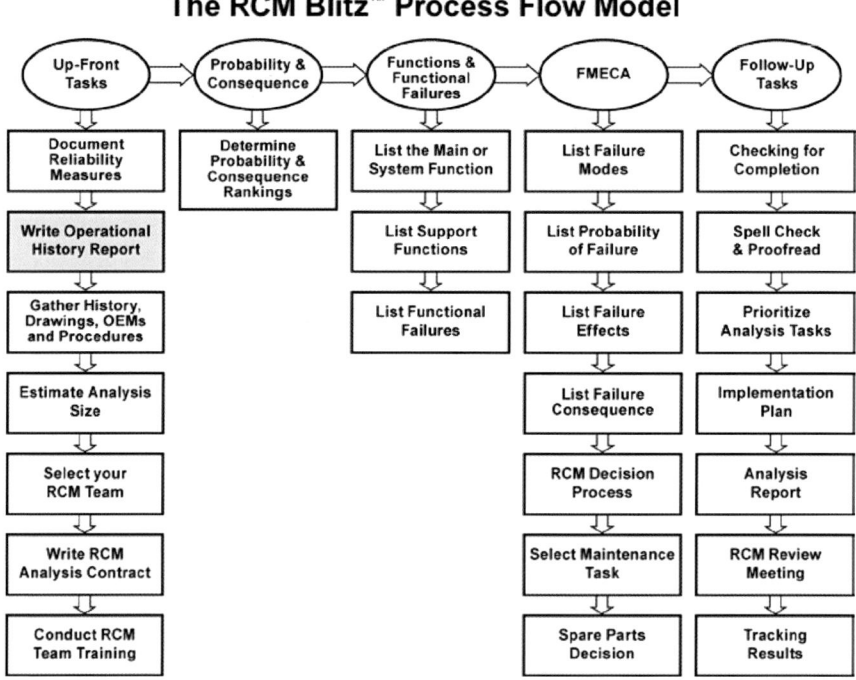

The second Up-Front task we need to complete is the Operational History Report. This report should be written by the RCM facilitator and a person who is considered an expert on the system you are about to analyze. (This is typically a process engineer who understands what the asset was designed to do, the expectations your business has for the asset, and how it is presently performing.)

The Operational History Report was created following several hour-long sessions to complete a main function statement. After going through this punishing event several times, it became clear that it is not uncommon for maintenance, operations, and engineering, to have a different perception of what a business expects from a given asset. It became evident that we needed to create a document to ground the RCM team on what a particular business expects from this critical asset.

The Operational History Report should be kept to less than two typewritten pages but should also clearly outline the context in which the equipment operates. The intent of this report is to provide the RCM team with a document that describes this critical asset and the performance expectations required from it on a daily basis. A well written Operational History Report will help your RCM team clearly understand the expectations of the asset at the start of your analysis and save time over the entire analysis. At a minimum, a good operational history report will include the following information:

- What is the designed function of this process?
- Why was it purchased?
- When was it installed?
- What performance standards do we expect this process to maintain?
- What is the present performance of this process?
- What is the consequence of down time?
- What are the costs of down time?
- What are the quality standards for this process?
- What are the health, safety, and environmental standards for this process?
- What is the standard operating procedure for this process?
- What are some common problems/failures that we have seen with this asset?
- What are the boundaries for this analysis?

Here is a sample Operational History Report:

Callahan Brewing Case Conveyor
The Callahan Brewing Case Conveyor was designed, purchased and installed in 1990. The system was designed to transport up to 1000 pounds of product at a rate of 120 feet per minute.

The case conveyor is powered by a variable-speed, five-horsepower, Reliance 240 volt AC motor. The motor is coupled to a 10:1 gearbox that in turn drives the conveyor via sprockets and chain. The chain drive is equipped with an auto-tensioner that keeps a constant tension on the drive chain. The tensioner is equipped with a broken-chain limit switch that immediately alarms the line operator of a broken-chain condition. The product being conveyed rides on a continuous belt that is connected at each end with metal lacing.

This conveyor is also equipped with a product-stopped photo eye (PE-1). The function of this eye is to stop the conveyor drive should the photo eye be blocked for longer than 30 seconds. Once the conveyor shuts down, the operator is again alarmed, and must reset the PLC to re-start the conveyor. This conveyor is critical to the operation of our business as it conveys finished product to the palletizer where it is then shipped for distribution to our customers. Down time of more than 15 minutes is unacceptable. At this time, there are no PM or PdM tasks in place. The four conveyors were seen as highly reliable in the first 7 to 8 years of service but over the past few years have been prone to major stoppages.

Quality is a top priority for Callahan Brewing, and as a result, we expect that every case that leaves this brewery will be free of any visible external damage and that all case openings will be completely sealed.

Future plans for our business show a twenty percent increase in thru-put over the next two years. This expected increase in thru-put would exceed, by 10%, the designed capability of these conveyors.

Major failures for the four product conveyors over the past three years have included two motor failures, one conveyance belt, one gearbox, and several drive-bearing failures. Persistent minor failures include drive chains, sprockets and gearbox seal leaks. Quality has also been a problem over the last several months as conveyor jams have resulted in over 100 damaged cases per week. Damaged cases and product must be destroyed to ensure customer safety.

There are very few Health, Safety, and Environmental concerns in regards to the case conveyor, but there is potential for incidents and accidents, including the hazards of operating rotating equipment (pinch points, entanglement), and minor oil or beer spills that could result in slips and falls.

Down time of the product conveyor results in a back-up of production. After ten minutes, the bottle filler associated with that conveyor will shut down, resulting in a loss of 75 cases of beer each minute. At this point in time, Callahan Brewing is in a sold-out position, so each lost case results in lost revenue of $5.00 per/case.

The boundaries of this RCM analysis will include the entire case conveyor, drive and starter.

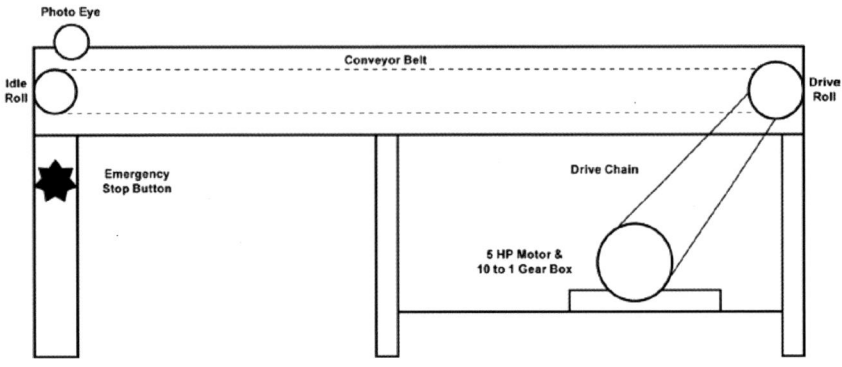

Up-Front Tasks
Gathering Information Necessary to Perform a RCM Analysis

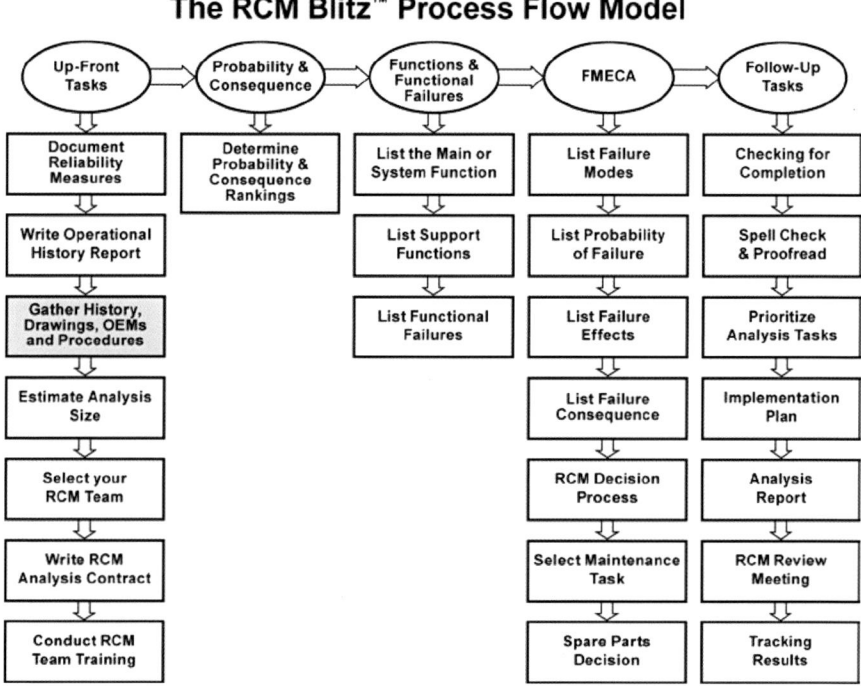

In preparation for you upcoming RCM analysis, you will need to gather some critical information and documents to assist your team in performing a thorough analysis. The results and accuracy of your analysis will be dependent on the accuracy of the information you present at the start of the analysis. Over the past fifteen years I have learned it is well worth the time it may take to gather and review this information prior to the start of each analysis. Below is a list of items to have on hand prior to the start of each analysis:

1. Drawings - I prefer P&ID's and ask a local expert to review and update the drawings prior to the start of the analysis if necessary.

2. A complete list of maintenance PM and PdM activities that are being performed on this asset. While we perform each analysis as if nothing is being done to maintain the asset, we do consider the value of each task that may be on that list.

3. OEM (Original Equipment Manufacturer) manuals for assets or components within the system you are analyzing.

4. Operations and Maintenance History - it's nice to have on hand a list of failures that have occurred on the asset, provided the information your company enters into the CMMS is accurate and available.

5. Control Logic - This helps the team determine accurate evidence/alarms for a detailed troubleshooting guide.

6. A complete list of all components within the boundaries of the RCM analysis. This can be created from the P&ID and/or a walk-down the equipment. (At a minimum this item is an absolute must!)

Over the years, these items have arrived in various forms, ranging from hopelessly inaccurate (a P&ID showing the last revision taking place in 1967, a date even prior to the development of RCM!) to totally non-existent. In the event this takes place, your job as the RCM facilitator has now become significantly more difficult. The lack of accurate information will slow the progress of the analysis and the accuracy of your final output. This also makes the selection of your RCM team extremely important, as each person will now need to truly know their portion of this asset from top to bottom.

In training and certifying facilitators over the years, nearly all have heard me say that lack of good information at the start of your analysis will always result in a large RCM parking lot. The parking lot of a RCM analysis contains unfinished failure modes that require additional work outside the analysis to determine accurate failure effects or failure symptoms.

Up-Front Tasks
Estimating the Size of Your RCM Analysis

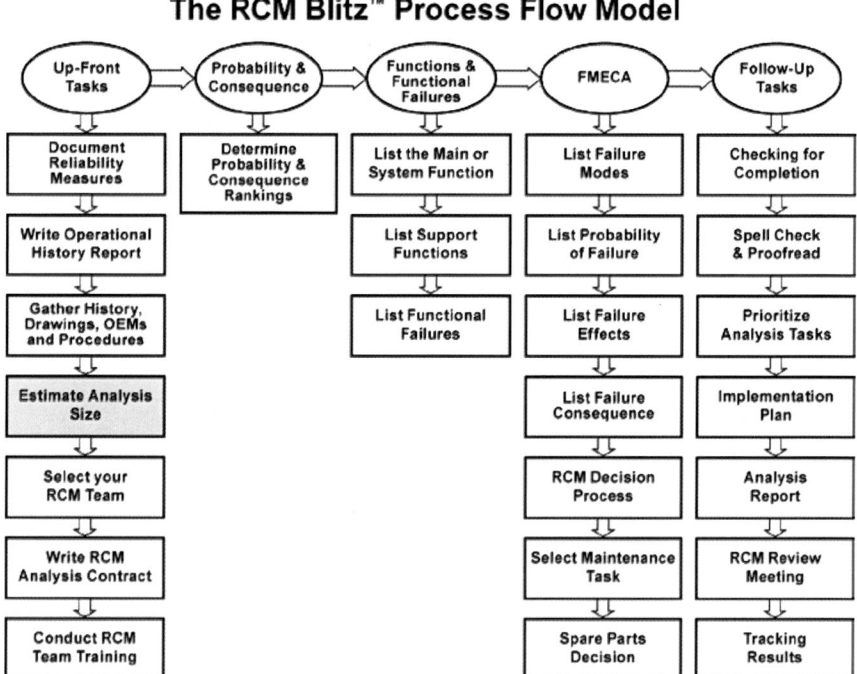

The RCM Blitz™ Process Flow Model

Now that you have selected a critical asset for analysis, and gathered drawings and documentation for your upcoming event, you will need to estimate the size of this RCM analysis. When I first developed RCM Blitz™, the goal of the process was to perform a quick, yet thorough, traditional RCM analysis on a critical asset or piece of equipment within the time limit of one week. While I now understand the value of Reliability Centered Maintenance and enjoyed facilitating analyses, the methodology I first learned took far too long to complete what I call the RCM Cycle. This cycle includes analysis preparation, training of participants, performing the RCM analysis and implementing the recommended tasks.

The largest part of the RCM Cycle prior to RCM Blitz™ was performing the RCM analysis itself. It was thought, at the time, that the best way to facilitate the process was to break the analysis up into several 2 or 4 hour meetings over several weeks time. As a result, it was not uncommon for the typical RCM analysis to take up to six months to complete. While this process added value, the managers I worked with, and the teams I lead, grew impatient with the time it took to complete the analysis itself. The 2 and 4 hour meeting format was developed following a paradigm that meetings lasting more than four hours were exhausting for both the facilitator and participants. Amazingly enough, those trained to facilitate a process that focuses on mitigating causes and effects had never looked to identify and eliminate the causes that led to traditional RCM taking so long.

With a clear goal in mind, we looked to identify and eliminate the causes leading to the lengthy time needed to complete a traditional RCM analysis (traditional RCM is any methodology that meets or exceeds the SAE RCM standard JA1011-12). In completing a review of the RCM process, we identified the following causes that slowed the process, making meetings slow and exhausting. For each cause we then identified the effects and then an action to eliminate each cause.

1. **Cause** – The job of facilitating RCM is too large for one facilitator

    Effects – A single facilitator can only work as fast as his brain and motor skills will allow and as a result the facilitator has to ask the required questions and then record the information he hears on the flip chart. This results in extended periods of silence, as well as constant review of dialog, to ensure the wording on the flip chart represents what the team has said.

    Action – Use co-facilitators to facilitate the RCM process. This allows one person to lead the group and the other to listen and record information. This eliminates half of the load on the facilitator's brain. Rather than thinking about what is the next step in the RCM process and how did the team answer the question, with co-facilitators, one facilitator focuses on the RCM process, and the other focuses on what the team is saying. Each hour the facilitators can change roles to keep the process moving and the team energized.

2. **Cause** – Writing all information on flip charts slows the process

    Effects – In writing all information on the flipchart, an excessive amount of time is wasted as the team waits for the facilitator to write out information. Additionally, the information recorded on the flipchart needs to be written clearly as it will be transferred to the software following the meeting.

Action – Develop a RCM database that can be used to record information as the analysis is being performed. While we were told that using software in the analysis slowed the process, a good database or software actually helps to improve the speed and accuracy of the analysis. Those with even average typing skills can record information on the computer much faster than one can write on the flipchart. Nearly fifteen years later, almost all RCM methodologies now use software to record information in the analysis.

3. **Cause** – The 2 to 4 hour meeting blocks result in continuous review of past information

    Effect – Chopping the analysis up into short meeting blocks results in a review of what has been covered so far and what is left to complete at each meeting.

    Action – We were confident that if we could keep up the pace of the meeting, the RCM team would remain engaged and the process would be less tiresome. We felt confident we could complete most analyses in five days, or less, if we scheduled the analyses for eight hours a day. The result was the birth of RCM Blitz™!

4. **Cause** – The analysis process is broken into too many parts and does not have a natural flow

    Effects – We had been trained to facilitate the process in several distinct steps, list all functions, list all functional failures, list all the failure modes, list all failure effects and then develop tasks for each failure mode. Performing the analysis in this manner, again, resulted in constant review. As an example, in the third week of the analysis we might list a failure mode, three weeks later we might list the failure effects for this failure mode, and then again four weeks later we would discuss the failure mode as we developed a task using the RCM decision process.

    Action – Continue to follow the required steps of traditional RCM but perform them in a way that flows more naturally. We made the decision to list functions first, then the functional failures for the main function only, then we move on to perform the FMECA (Failure Modes and Effects Criticality Analysis) portion of the analysis in continuous loops. Example: We list the failure mode, discuss the effects of that mode, immediately develop a task, and, having completed that failure mode, we move on to the next one.

Implementing each of the above actions we now needed to be able to estimate what can be completed in a week long RCM Blitz event. Looking at our past RCM schedules we felt comfortable that we could reduce the total time (Add up all the two and four hour meetings and come up with total time it took to complete each analysis) by as much as 40%. Using that figure we estimated that we could complete a RCM analysis that covered 85 to 100 components and 120 to 140 failure modes in 1 week. With those numbers as our goal we can now develop estimates for the number of functions and failure modes within the boundaries of our analysis.

I thought after nearly fifteen years of facilitating RCM Blitz™ analyses it would be nice to include what an experienced RCM Blitz™ facilitator and team can complete over five days meeting 8 hours a day. In the last two years with our new RCM Blitz™ software on more than ten separate locations with different RCM teams, we have had facilitators complete analyses that covered over 200 components and over 300 failure modes. Experience and patience are king when to comes to building speed and efficiency!

Estimating Functions
Using the component list you created in gathering information for the analysis, count the number of components on the list and multiply that number by 1.5, this will be the estimated number of functions in your analysis. The number of functions is larger than the number of components because some components have more than one function. A continuous level device, for example, may have to meet the requirement of providing a signal for tank level as well as be able to detect and alarm tank-high level conditions.

Estimating Failure Modes
As a general rule, we can estimate the number of failure modes in a RCM analysis by multiplying the number of components by 3. Using these numbers as a reference, you should easily be able to complete an analysis within five days.

Common Failure Modes for Estimating Analysis Size:

- **Motor Failures - 5**
    - Motor bearing fails due to contamination.
    - Motor bearing fails due to lack of lubrication.
    - Motor bearing fails due to over lubrication.
    - Motor windings fail due to normal wear.
    - Motor bearing fails due to misalignment.

- **Couplings - 2**
    - Coupling fails due to misalignment.
    - Coupling fails due to lack of lubrication.

- **Pumps - 11**
    - Pump bearing fails due to contamination.
    - Pump bearing fails due to lack of lubrication.
    - Pump bearing fails due to misalignment.
    - Pump bearing fails due to improper installation.
    - Pump seal fails due to misalignment.
    - Pump seal fails due to improper installation.
    - Pump seal flush is plugged.
    - Pump impeller fails due to normal wear.
    - Pump impeller fails due to corrosion/erosion.
    - Pump impeller fails due to jammed foreign object.
    - Pump bearing/seal/coupling fails due to soft foot condition.

- **Gearbox - 3**
    - Gearbox fails due to lack of lubrication.
    - Gearbox fails due to oil contamination.
    - Gearbox fails due to normal wear.

- **Starters - 2**
    - Starter fails due to lost contact/connection.
    - Starter fails due to worn contact.

- **Valves - 4**

    - Valve fails in the open position.
    - Valve fails in the closed position.
    - Valve body seal fails due to normal wear.
    - Valve packing fails due to normal wear.

- **Switches (Limit, Flow, Pressure, Level, Photo Eyes, etc.) - 3**

    - Switch fails open - random.
    - Switch fails closed - random.
    - Switch fails out of adjustment.

- **Chains - 4**

    - Chain worn due to abrasion.
    - Chain fails due to misalignment.
    - Chain fails due to improper installation.
    - Chain fails due to lack of lubrication.

- **Sprockets - 3**

    - Sprocket worn due to abrasion.
    - Sprocket fails due to improper chain tension.
    - Sprocket fails due to misalignment.

- **Belts - 3**

    - Belt worn due to abrasion.
    - Belt fails due to misalignment.
    - Belt fails due to improper installation (tension).

- **Sheaves - 3**

    - Sheave worn due to abrasion.
    - Sheave fails due to misalignment.
    - Sheave fails due to improper installation.

- **Equipment Guarding - 2**

    - Guarding fails due to being left off.
    - Guarding fails due to insufficient coverage.

- **Actuators - 4**
    - Actuator seal leaks due to normal wear.
    - Actuator seal leaks due to scored shaft.
    - Actuator mounting hardware fails due to torque/vibration.
    - Actuator seal leaks due to lack of lubrication.

- **Solenoids - 2**
    - Solenoid fails open – random.
    - Solenoid fails closed – random.

- **Piping - 4**
    - Piping worn due to abrasion.
    - Piping fails due to corrosion/erosion.
    - Piping fails due to improper support.
    - Piping fails due to external damage.

- **Tanks/Vessels - 3**
    - Tank fails due to normal wear.
    - Tank fails due to corrosion/erosion.
    - Tank fails due to external damage.

Up-Front Tasks
Selecting and Training Your RCM Team

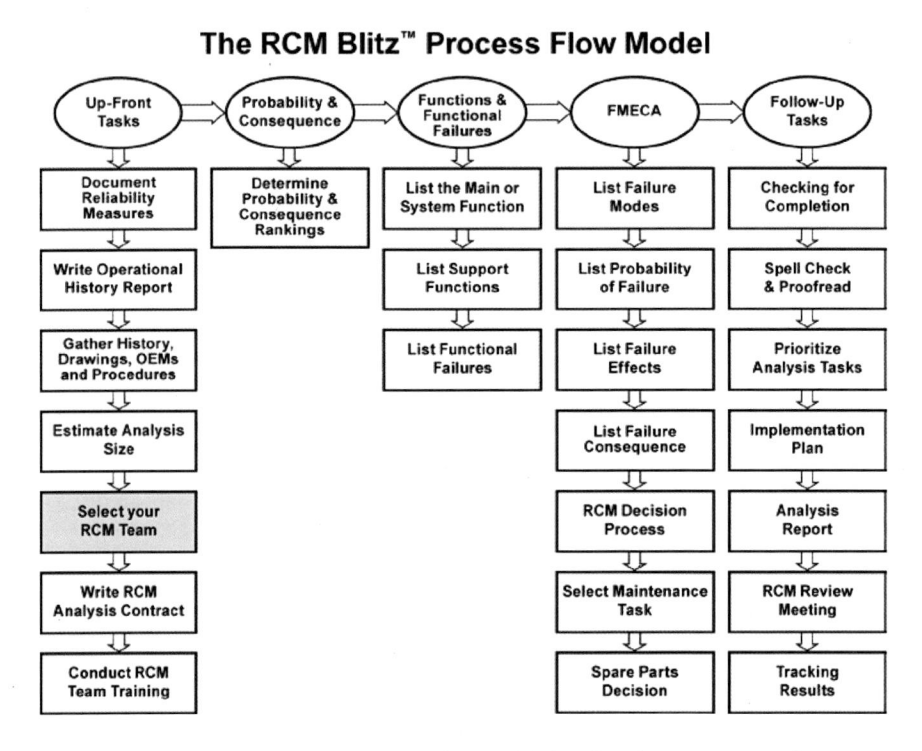

The RCM Blitz™ Process Flow Model

Up-Front Tasks	Probability & Consequence	Functions & Functional Failures	FMECA	Follow-Up Tasks
Document Reliability Measures	Determine Probability & Consequence Rankings	List the Main or System Function	List Failure Modes	Checking for Completion
Write Operational History Report		List Support Functions	List Probability of Failure	Spell Check & Proofread
Gather History, Drawings, OEMs and Procedures		List Functional Failures	List Failure Effects	Prioritize Analysis Tasks
Estimate Analysis Size			List Failure Consequence	Implementation Plan
Select your RCM Team			RCM Decision Process	Analysis Report
Write RCM Analysis Contract			Select Maintenance Task	RCM Review Meeting
Conduct RCM Team Training			Spare Parts Decision	Tracking Results

At first glance, RCM appears to be a fairly simple process. The SAE standard for RCM outlines a seven-step structured process. A quick review of the seven steps might lead one to believe that any idiot off the street could, within a matter of an hour or two, simply follow the steps and participate in or facilitate the process. While I wish it were that simple, I like to describe RCM as a simple process containing many subtle but complex elements. When facilitated correctly by a seasoned practitioner, and a team of expert participants, RCM appears to be both easy and fun. I like to tell people that I love my job because it is so easy. I follow a step-by-step process, ask lots of questions and I'm not required to know anything about the clients equipment or process. RCM is easy!

While the process may seem simple at first glance, companies who have successful RCM efforts understand it requires expertise at two levels: the RCM facilitator and the RCM team.

This section will focus on how to build a team of RCM participants who will be charged with completing a thorough analysis that will deliver the maintenance and operational tasks required to ensure the inherent designed reliability of your assets.

The Make-up of a Great RCM Team
In order to get the best results from each RCM analysis, you will need to select a cross-functional team of expert participants with representatives from operations, maintenance, engineering and predictive technologies.

The typical make-up of a RCM team includes the following people:

1. **Maintenance Craft People** - with representatives from mechanical, electrical and instrumentation. Your maintenance craft people will provide information on possible failure modes and are critical in making task decisions.

2. **Operations** - Every RCM analysis MUST have one or two experienced operators. While this process is named Reliability Centered Maintenance, your deliverability will be incomplete without representation from operations. Equipment operators live with your assets on a day-to-day basis. The experience they have in operating the equipment, and the failures they have witnessed over the years, will provide some of the most valuable information necessary to complete a good analysis. Operators provide the most accurate information when it comes to failure effects and failure symptoms.

3. **Predictive Maintenance Technician** - The PdM technician is necessary in helping to determine what tools can be used to detect potential failures on failure modes that have a useful P-F interval. They also provide recommendations for precision maintenance techniques that can eliminate failure modes or drastically improve MTBF (Mean Time Between Failures) for many failure modes.

4. **Process Engineer** - This is the engineer who's responsibility is the asset being analyzed. This person will provide information on how the asset is supposed to perform and the potential consequences to your business should it fail.

Each person on the RCM team should be considered an expert by their peers on the process or asset you are analyzing. Along with being considered an expert, each individual should be open to change as well as new ideas and concepts. As you select your participants, consider each person and their demonstrated abilities when it comes to troubleshooting failures AND to applying corrective actions that eliminate them from occurring again.

Outside the RCM facilitator and the team participants, you should also consider part-time daily representation from both operations and maintenance supervision and management. As a practitioner, I would never expect managers to sit through an entire RCM analysis, but it is important for them to sit in for an hour or so each day to monitor progress of the event, answer questions that may have come up in the analysis and, most importantly, show support for the process and the team.

I would like to offer caution when it comes to the size of your RCM team. The best teams contain representatives from each of the required areas and are made up of 5 to 8 people. There is always the temptation to add people to the RCM team with the belief that more people adds more experience, along with the thought that the more people exposed to RCM concepts the better. Large teams can slow the process and make the job of the facilitators more difficult. When starting out your RCM team, I would urge you to maintain the minimum numbers. As the RCM culture and expertise begins to take hold in your company, you can add more people to the analysis. The best way to manage this is to consult with your facilitators before you add additional representatives.

Training RCM Participants
While there are varying thoughts on how much training RCM participants should receive, the intent of your RCM Participant training should focus on the elements required to make the team effective participants.

The RCM Blitz™ Participant Training is a four-hour training module that is focused on instructing participants in RCM terminology and the RCM process flow. Simply put, only your facilitators need to be considered experts in regards to the RCM process, the team will learn the information required to participate during the training and then learn the remaining concepts as they participate in the analysis.

Up- Front Tasks
The RCM Analysis Contract

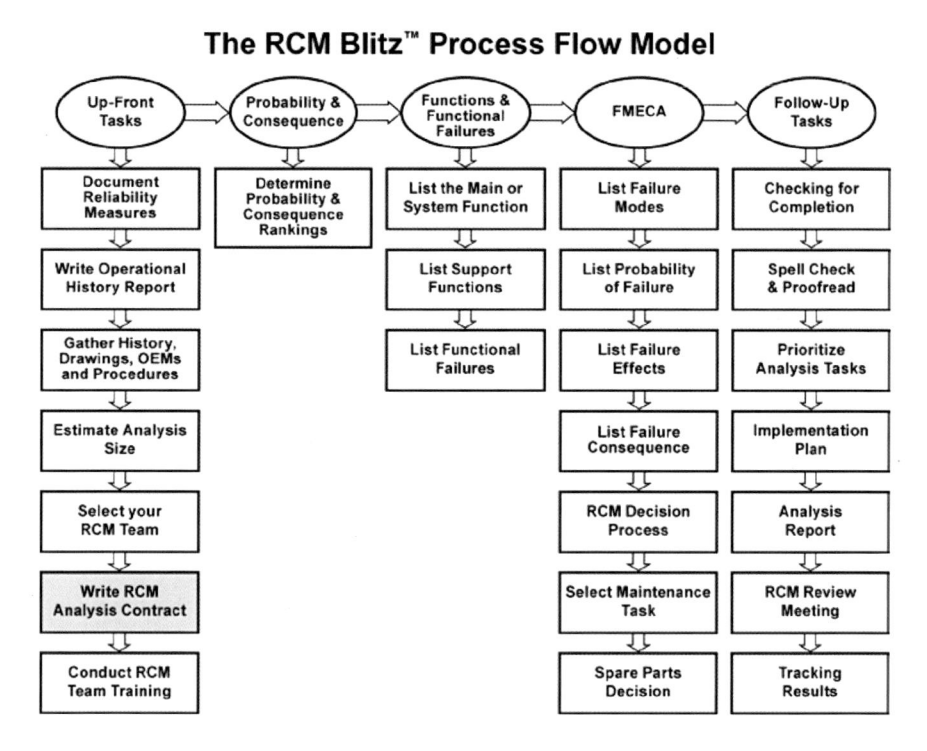

The RCM Blitz™ Process Flow Model

Up-Front Tasks	Probability & Consequence	Functions & Functional Failures	FMECA	Follow-Up Tasks
Document Reliability Measures	Determine Probability & Consequence Rankings	List the Main or System Function	List Failure Modes	Checking for Completion
Write Operational History Report		List Support Functions	List Probability of Failure	Spell Check & Proofread
Gather History, Drawings, OEMs and Procedures		List Functional Failures	List Failure Effects	Prioritize Analysis Tasks
Estimate Analysis Size			List Failure Consequence	Implementation Plan
Select your RCM Team			RCM Decision Process	Analysis Report
Write RCM Analysis Contract			Select Maintenance Task	RCM Review Meeting
Conduct RCM Team Training			Spare Parts Decision	Tracking Results

Those who know me, or have spent enough time working with me, have probably heard me say, at one time or another, that I am not the smartest person in the world but I am capable of learning if I make the same mistake enough times. This is how the RCM analysis contract came to be a valuable step in the RCM Blitz™ process. Anyone who has ever had to set up the logistics for a meeting should have a good understanding of the complications that arise when trying to secure a conference room for a week, deal with the conflicts of inviting several people, ensure that all invited show up at the correct place at the right time, and that all the equipment and information for the meeting is there as well. Scheduling and preparing for a RCM analysis can be a nightmare!

When I first started using the RCM Blitz™ process at Kodak, scheduling and preparation were easy because there was not a huge demand to tie up key people for a full week. We had to beg people to volunteer for the first few pilot analyses. Following the success of these analyses however, word quickly spread about the process and soon demand to perform RCM's reached a point where two people were not going to be enough to satisfy the demand. We would send a note to the area sponsoring the analysis asking for a conference room, easel, note pads, digital projector and to make sure the people needed in the RCM were invited. Needless to say, this system of sending e-mails worked about as well as a bottomless bucket for holding water. It seemed that for nearly every RCM we did we encountered one problem or another regarding the conference room, invitees, materials or documents. The end result was severe frustration on the part of the RCM facilitators, RCM teams and sponsoring managers. It was time once again to review the relationship of cause and effect!

1. **Effect** - People invited to the RCM did not show up.

   Cause - They were not on the e-mail distribution list, or were not scheduled to be working that shift.

2. **Effect** - The conference room selected was too small, we did not have enough chairs for the people invited and there was not enough room on the wall to support RCM documents.

   Cause - We were not specific regarding the size of the conference room we needed.

3. **Effect** - We did not have the documents and drawings needed to perform the analysis at the beginning of the week.

   Cause - We did not specify that we must have specific information to perform the analysis.

After reviewing the causes of RCM analysis interruption, we determined that while we were getting good at following a structured process, we were miserable when it came to planning and scheduling RCM events! In the end, we took two hours and developed a process for planning and scheduling our RCM analyses.

This process is the RCM Contract. This contract is a formal document that lists all the requirements needed to perform a good RCM analysis.

It includes:

- Who needs to attend
- Requirements of the meeting room (including size, number of seats, and materials needed for facilitation)
- Who is the sponsor of the analysis

- The dates and times the team will meet
- The documents and information needed for the RCM and people charged with providing this information

Once we had created a list of all the things we needed, we added the deliverables our sponsor could expect from the analysis and what they should expect from the RCM facilitators.

Our initial thought was that we would e-mail this document to the analysis sponsor and our life would be fantastic from that day forward. The reality was, while the contract offered some improvement, we still encountered simple problems that upset the process. In the end, we made the decision to deliver the contract by hand to the analysis sponsor, have them sign the document and then obtain the signatures of all involved in the RCM analysis.

By adding the signatures, we now had a process that worked like a Swiss watch, our analyses went off without fault, as planned and scheduled!

To this date, the RCM contract is listed as a critical and necessary step in the RCM Blitz™ process flow. I can also say that most facilitators attempt to skip this critical step of the process and in the end learn the same thing I did. If you fail to spend the time to properly plan your analysis, you will lose up to five times that amount, compensating for your poor planning.

Simply put, by signing the contract, people remember what their responsibilities are regarding the RCM analysis and the process works.

A Sample RCM Contract

TO:	***NAME, TITLE***
FROM:	***YOUR NAME***, RCM Facilitator
SUBJECT:	RCM Analysis Contract for ***INSERT EQUIPMENT NAME***

On ***INSERT DATES***, an RCM analysis will be performed on ***INSERT EQUIPMENT NAME*** located in ***INSERT EQUIPMENT LOCATION***.

The RCM facilitator will provide the following:

- Training for the RCM participants
- Facilitation of a complete RCM analysis which includes:
    - Function of equipment
    - Functional failures
    - Complete maintenance strategy
    - Spare parts strategy
- Prioritization of RCM tasks
- Assistance in the development of an implementation strategy

The RCM Analysis Sponsor will provide:

- An RCM analysis implementation manager
- A room to conduct the RCM analysis (Specify Room Size)
- Uninterrupted time of the RCM team for the length of the analysis

Together, the facilitator and RCM Analysis Sponsor will provide:

- A complete operational history report
- The names of individuals selected to participate in the analysis
- Drawings, procedures, and equipment history needed for the analysis

X_____
RCM Facilitator

X_____
RCM Analysis Sponsor

X_____
Analysis Implementation Manager

X_____

X_____

X_____

X_____

X_____
RCM Team Members

Up-Front Tasks
Train Your RCM Team

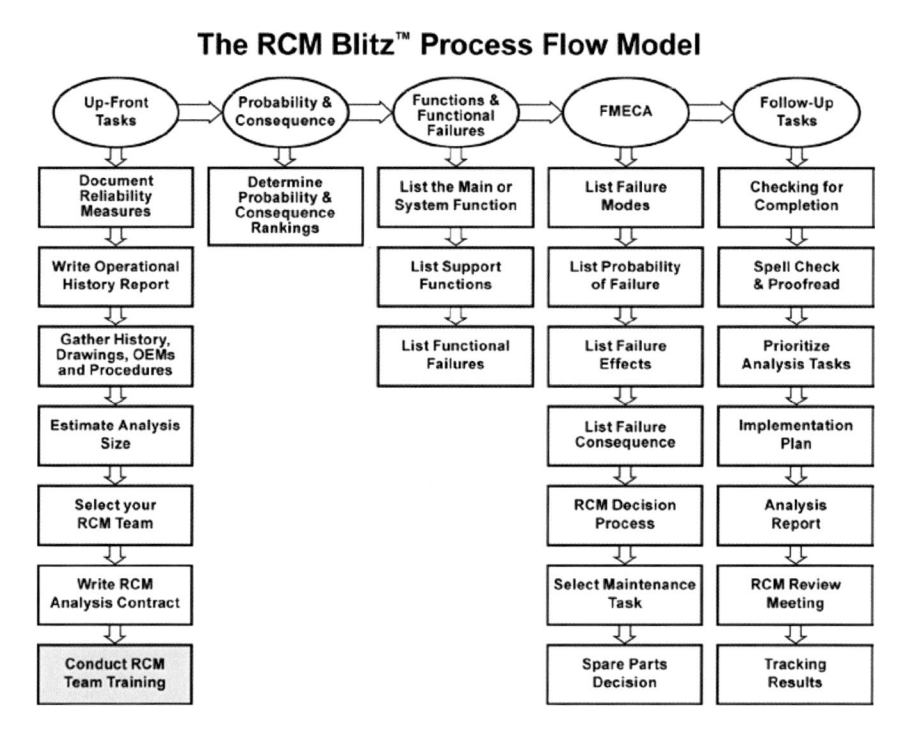

The RCM Blitz™ Process Flow Model

```
┌──────────┐   ┌──────────────┐   ┌──────────────┐   ┌────────┐   ┌──────────┐
│ Up-Front │ → │ Probability &│ → │ Functions &  │ → │ FMECA  │ → │ Follow-Up│
│  Tasks   │   │ Consequence  │   │ Functional   │   │        │   │  Tasks   │
│          │   │              │   │  Failures    │   │        │   │          │
└──────────┘   └──────────────┘   └──────────────┘   └────────┘   └──────────┘
```

Up-Front Tasks	Probability & Consequence	Functions & Functional Failures	FMECA	Follow-Up Tasks
Document Reliability Measures	Determine Probability & Consequence Rankings	List the Main or System Function	List Failure Modes	Checking for Completion
Write Operational History Report		List Support Functions	List Probability of Failure	Spell Check & Proofread
Gather History, Drawings, OEMs and Procedures		List Functional Failures	List Failure Effects	Prioritize Analysis Tasks
Estimate Analysis Size			List Failure Consequence	Implementation Plan
Select your RCM Team			RCM Decision Process	Analysis Report
Write RCM Analysis Contract			Select Maintenance Task	RCM Review Meeting
Conduct RCM Team Training			Spare Parts Decision	Tracking Results

About three or four years ago, I had a RCM facilitator inform me that he would be training his RCM Team on Friday afternoon, and when I got to the plant the following Monday, the team would be trained and ready to jump right into the RCM analysis. The idea sounded good to me. I had seen him perform part of the training course at facilitator training and he had done quite well. When I showed up the following Monday, my friend jumped right into reviewing the Operational History Report and began working with his team to list main and support functions. By that afternoon, we were ready to jump into the FMECA (Failure Modes and Effects Criticality Analysis). As soon as we began to discuss the first failure mode, it was evident this team had never been trained. The RCM stalled, the facilitator, as well as the team, was lost. I let them flounder for an hour before I began asking questions, including, "I'm guessing that your team never went through the RCM Blitz™ Participant training?"

Answer: "Well we had a major breakdown Friday afternoon and I just figured we could get by without the training."

The intent of the RCM Blitz™ Participant training course is to provide enough instruction in RCM language and techniques to make the team effective participants. Not RCM experts! A good facilitator can accomplish this in less than 4 hours, and it works best when you instruct the course immediately before starting a RCM analysis. When your RCM team finishes their first analysis, they will be leaps and bounds ahead of what most people know about the RCM process.

CHAPTER 3
Probability and Consequence

Probability & Consequence Rankings

The RCM Blitz™ Process Flow Model

```
Up-Front Tasks → Probability & Consequence → Functions & Functional Failures → FMECA → Follow-Up Tasks
```

Up-Front Tasks	Probability & Consequence	Functions & Functional Failures	FMECA	Follow-Up Tasks
Document Reliability Measures	Determine Probability & Consequence Rankings	List the Main or System Function	List Failure Modes	Checking for Completion
Write Operational History Report		List Support Functions	List Probability of Failure	Spell Check & Proofread
Gather History, Drawings, OEMs and Procedures		List Functional Failures	List Failure Effects	Prioritize Analysis Tasks
Estimate Analysis Size			List Failure Consequence	Implementation Plan
Select your RCM Team			RCM Decision Process	Analysis Report
Write RCM Analysis Contract			Select Maintenance Task	RCM Review Meeting
Conduct RCM Team Training			Spare Parts Decision	Tracking Results

When I first began performing RCM analyses at Eastman Kodak, we never discussed the probability that each failure would occur nor the consequences to our business should the failure occur. At the end of these analyses, we would often have over 100 tasks that needed to be implemented. It was at this point that we would begin to struggle with what should we do first? As a result, the implementation of the RCM tasks that resulted from our first analyses became a difficult proposition. This difficulty was compounded by the fact that we were limited by the number of people available to perform these tasks. From each RCM analysis, it is not uncommon to have as many as one hundred and fifty tasks that require people to write maintenance PM and PdM procedures, operating procedures, start-up and product change procedures, management of change documents as well as the follow-up of recommended redesigns. With a list of 150 items, where does one begin? We needed to develop a process to rank the importance of each task.

In the RCM process, tasks are developed to mitigate the consequences of each failure mode and, as a result, a process is needed to rank the potential consequences of each failure and the likelihood or probability of each failure occurring. Understanding each failure mode will result in a corresponding task. In combining the probability of each failure, and the consequence of each failure, we can then derive a criticality ranking.

Probability of Failure
When we look to rank the probability of each failure mode, we are making an assessment of the likelihood this failure will occur, based on the past history, or experience, of the RCM team. For each RCM analysis, we create a document that sets clear boundaries of what constitutes a High, Medium or Low probability failure mode. The RCM facilitator will first list the Main Function, and all of the Support Functions, for each component within the boundaries of the RCM analysis. We then ask the team to highlight the top ten components that fail most often and ask the question, "How often do these failures occur?"

The goal is to set a cut-off point for High probability failures that captures no more than the top twenty percent of our up-coming failure modes. With this step complete, we can now generate the criteria for High, Medium and Low priority.

Probability of Failure:
- **High - This failure mode occurs 1 time in 3 months or more frequently**
- **Medium - This failure mode has occurred before**
- **Low - This failure mode has never occurred**

Consequence of Failure
Following the development of failure mode probability criteria, we immediately move on to set the criteria for the consequence of each failure mode. As we rank the consequence of each failure mode, we assess the potential cost impact to our business with regards to the following criteria.

1. **Health, Safety, and Environment** - I would like to suggest that you consider any failure mode that could affect employee health, safety or environment a high consequence of failure. In recognizing

this, it elevates the potential mitigating tasks to a level that will ensure implementation. Splitting hairs on whether a potential spill will be less than 1 gallon, or more than 50, or whether an employee will be cut, or maimed, is dangerous and only slows the RCM process.

2. **Equipment Down Time** - To set the High consequence criteria for equipment downtime, we look to identify a set number of hours where, should this failure occur, the resulting downtime will result in severe consequences. Remembering that we perform RCM on the top twenty percent of the most critical assets, failure modes that result in the loss of these assets, and the products they produce, for some period of time should be painful. To come up with this number, I typically ask questions to find out how long this equipment can be down before there is danger of missing a shipment and at what point will upper management, or corporate headquarters, need to be notified that this critical asset is not running? Once we have determined the High consequence criteria, the medium and low rankings become easy.

3. **Impact on Product Quality** - Product quality criteria, in most cases, is predetermined by a company's quality organization. If not, we again ask a series of questions to determine an unacceptable level of product loss, or rework, that may result from a given failure mode. In the event a company does not have a predetermined unacceptable number or percent for quality losses, the process can be simplified by discussing the cost of poor quality. What is the financial impact of 1% off spec product? What is the cost of the raw materials to make the product, and how much time does it take to make 1%?

4. **Total Cost of Failure** - Total cost of failure takes into consideration for each failure mode, the cost of lost product, the cost of maintenance, and the cost of replacement parts. Prior to starting a RCM analysis, ask management to set the dollar amount that constitutes a High consequence to the business. From this number we then set dollar amounts for Medium, and Low consequence failures.

5. **Impact on Efficiency/Energy Usage** - It's very rare to have efficiency losses end up in the High consequence category but they can add up. I performed a RCM for a company on a compressed air system that had primary and stand-by air compressors and air

dryers. While the system was designed to run on a single compressor and dryer, years of neglect forced them to run both compressors and both dryers. **As a result, the failure** of a single compressor was now enough to shut down several key assets. The resulting RCM tasks brought the system back in control, but as we performed the analysis it was often discussed that we could mitigate some failures by again starting both compressors! To deter this action, the team calculated the inefficiency of running both units and the cost easily exceeded our total cost criteria for Low consequence failures. Inefficient operation can also be defined by the need for additional resources/people to operate, having to slow your equipment, or start and stop your equipment to make product. Following is an example of a consequence criteria document:

Consequence of Failure

High

- **Failure Mode affects employee health, safety or environment**
- **Failure Mode results in equipment downtime exceeding 4 hours**
- **Failure Mode results in the manufacturing of off spec product exceeding 2%**
- **Failure Mode results in a total cost exceeding $25,000**

Medium

- **Failure Mode does NOT affect employee health, safety or environment**
- **Failure Mode results in less than 4 hours of equipment downtime**
- **Failure Mode results in off spec product less than 2%**
- **Failure Mode results in total cost of less than $25,000**
- **Failure Mode results in inefficient operation of equipment at a cost greater than low consequence criteria**

Low

- **Failure Mode does NOT affect employee health, safety or environment**
- **Failure Mode results in less than 15 minutes of equipment downtime**

- **Failure Mode does not impact product quality**
- **Failure Mode results in total cost of less than $500.00**

Now that we have determined the criteria for ranking the probability and consequence of each failure mode, determining the criticality of failure mode and the priority of the resulting tasks becomes simple. To do this we use the matrix that follows.

Failure Modes that have a High probability of occurring, and High consequence to your business should they occur, have a criticality ranking of 1 and the resulting task will be considered priority 1. A failure mode with a Low probability of occurrence and a Medium consequence to your business should it occur, will receive a criticality ranking of 4 and the resulting tasks will receive a priority 4 rank.

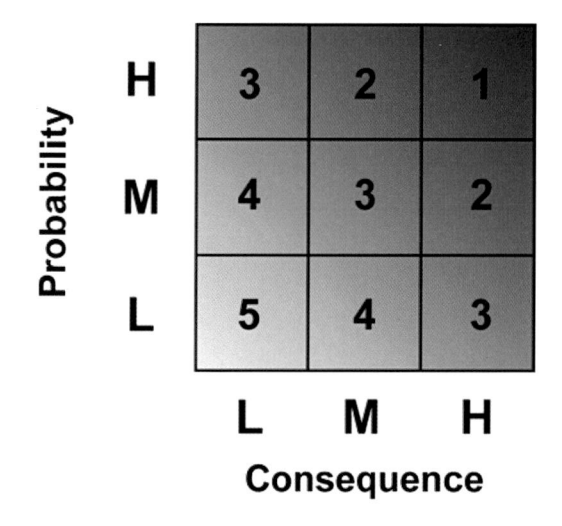

	L	M	H
H	3	2	1
M	4	3	2
L	5	4	3

Probability (vertical axis) / Consequence (horizontal axis)

CHAPTER 4
Functions and Functional Failures

Main or System Functions

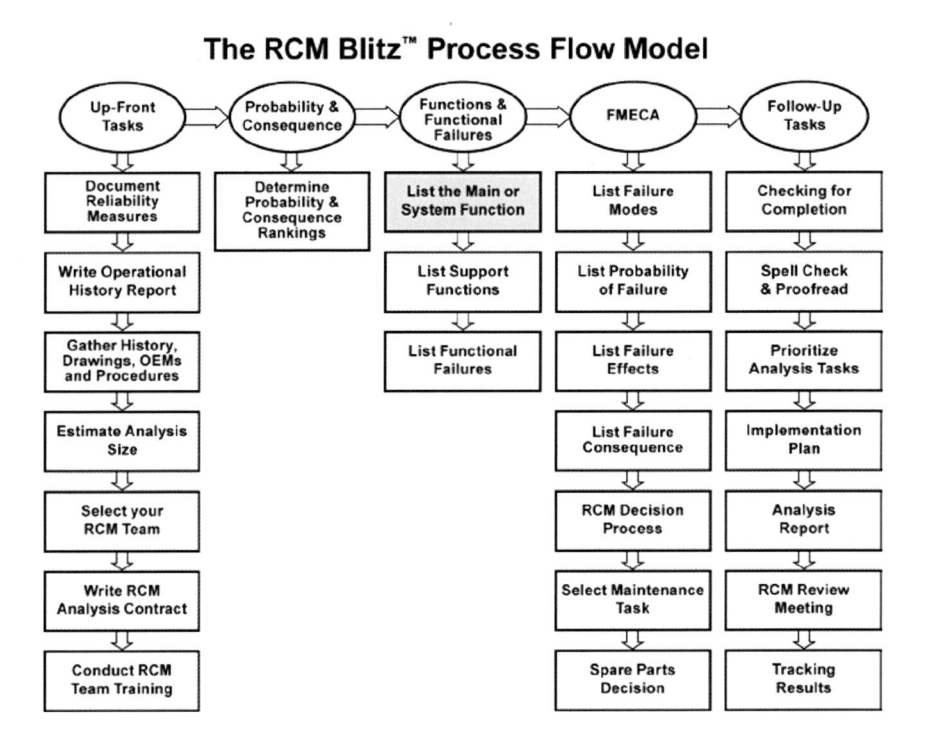

The RCM Blitz™ Process Flow Model

```
Up-Front Tasks → Probability & Consequence → Functions & Functional Failures → FMECA → Follow-Up Tasks
```

Up-Front Tasks	Probability & Consequence	Functions & Functional Failures	FMECA	Follow-Up Tasks
Document Reliability Measures	Determine Probability & Consequence Rankings	List the Main or System Function	List Failure Modes	Checking for Completion
Write Operational History Report		List Support Functions	List Probability of Failure	Spell Check & Proofread
Gather History, Drawings, OEMs and Procedures		List Functional Failures	List Failure Effects	Prioritize Analysis Tasks
Estimate Analysis Size			List Failure Consequence	Implementation Plan
Select your RCM Team			RCM Decision Process	Analysis Report
Write RCM Analysis Contract			Select Maintenance Task	RCM Review Meeting
Conduct RCM Team Training			Spare Parts Decision	Tracking Results

Identifying and listing equipment functions is the first step of the RCM Blitz™ analysis process. At this point, the RCM facilitators will begin working with the RCM team to list the Main Function of the asset, and then, the Support Functions for all the components within the boundaries of the analysis. This list of function statements will create the road map to a successful RCM analysis.

Listing the functions for each analysis is the first test of patience and leadership for every RCM facilitator. While listing functions typically takes less than four hours for a week-long RCM event, the identification and listing of the main and support functions can be painful.

Main Functions

The first function we look to identify with the RCM team is the Main Function. The Main Function is the reason the process, or piece of equipment, exists and the performance standards we expect the equipment to maintain. If the RCM facilitator and RCM analysis sponsor have done a good job in writing the Operational History Report, writing the Main Function statement should be very easy. It is highly important at this stage of the process to understand the importance of writing a clear and concise Main Function statement. This first statement, combined with the Support Functions, will dictate the depth and accuracy of your entire RCM analysis.

Looking at the definition of a Main Function statement, we can break the statement into two separate parts, the first being why do we own this asset, and the second being the performance standards we expect it to maintain. In drafting the first part of the Main Function statement, ask the team, "Why do we own this asset? At a basic level, what do we need this asset to do?"

For the Callahan Brewing beer conveyor, we need the conveyor to be able to convey cases of beer. This is the reason the conveyor was purchased. The Main Function statement for this asset would begin with the phrase:

To be able to convey cases of beer

The second part of the main function statement is the performance standards we expect the asset to maintain. The performance standards describe the standards we need this asset to maintain, on a day to day basis, in order to meet our business goals. This would include items such as the rate it needs to operate at, as well as the quality, health, safety and environmental standards we expect the asset to maintain. Again, if we have done a good job in writing the Operational History, determining the required performance standards should be fairly easy.

For the Callahan Brewing beer conveyor, we know why we have the asset, now we need to identify the performance standards we expect the asset to maintain.

In reviewing the Operational History Report, we can identify the following requirements as performance standards for the conveyor:

1. It needs to convey 1,000 pounds of product
2. It needs to operate at a rate of 132 feet/min (120 ft/min plus 10%)
3. It needs to maintain quality standards
4. It needs to maintain all Health, Safety and Environmental standards

Knowing this information we can now complete the Main Function statement for the Callahan Brewing beer conveyor - **To be able to convey 1,000 pounds of beer cases at a rate of 132 feet per minute while maintaining all quality, health, safety and environmental standards.**

Functions and Functional Failures
Support Functions

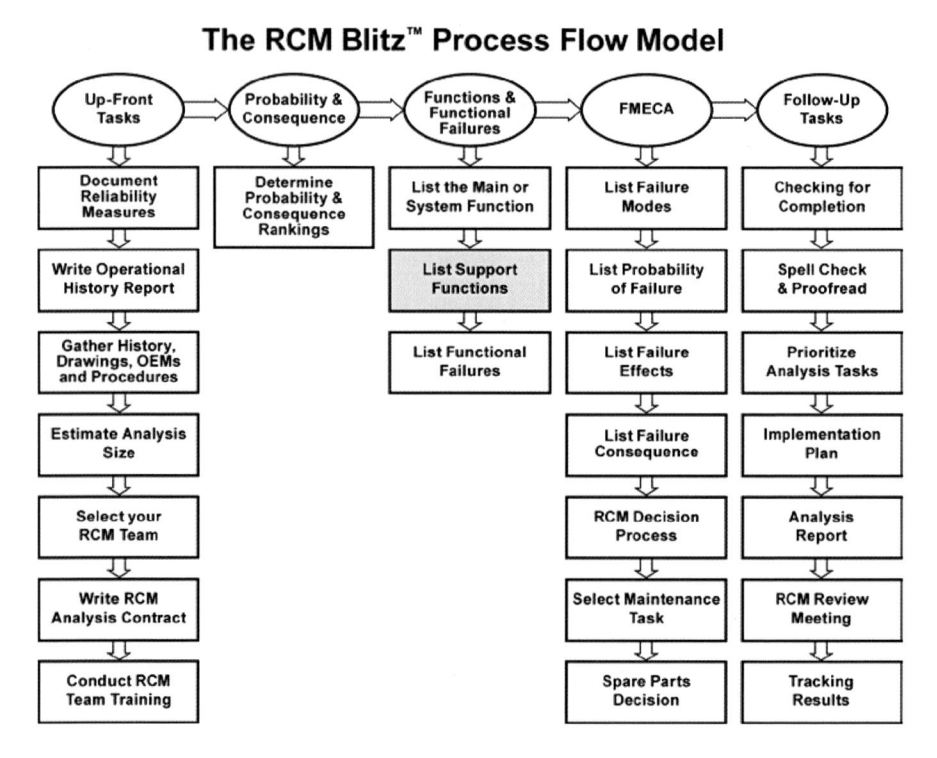

The RCM Blitz™ Process Flow Model

Up-Front Tasks	Probability & Consequence	Functions & Functional Failures	FMECA	Follow-Up Tasks
Document Reliability Measures	Determine Probability & Consequence Rankings	List the Main or System Function	List Failure Modes	Checking for Completion
Write Operational History Report		**List Support Functions**	List Probability of Failure	Spell Check & Proofread
Gather History, Drawings, OEMs and Procedures		List Functional Failures	List Failure Effects	Prioritize Analysis Tasks
Estimate Analysis Size			List Failure Consequence	Implementation Plan
Select your RCM Team			RCM Decision Process	Analysis Report
Write RCM Analysis Contract			Select Maintenance Task	RCM Review Meeting
Conduct RCM Team Training			Spare Parts Decision	Tracking Results

Once the Main Function of the RCM analysis has been determined, we move on to describe the support functions. In simple terms, the Support Functions describe, at a high level, the functionality of each component within the boundaries of the RCM analysis. In recognizing that listing functions can be painful (RCM teams tend to love discussing how things can fail yet seem to struggle in describing what we need each component to do), I looked for a simple way to accomplish two basic goals in terms of functionality:

1. Create a complete list that describes the basic function of each component within the boundaries of the analysis.

2. Develop a technique to identify potential Hidden Function Components early on in the RCM process.

Recognizing that the components that make up each asset are designed in some way to support the Main Function of the asset, we can now accomplish the first goal in describing Support Functions. In preparation for the RCM analysis, we created a list of components to estimate the size and time it would take to perform the RCM. We can now use this list to list the component, and its basic function.

The second goal, identifying potential Hidden Function components, is accomplished by asking one simple question as we identify the support functions of each component, "Is the component active or passive?"

Active Function Components
Active Function Components are components that perform an Active Function and do so each time the equipment is operated. During the normal operating condition of this asset, this component will be actively performing its intended function. As an example, a pump is a component that provides an active function. We describe Active Function components with the phrase "To be able to".

Examples of Active Function Components:

- Cooling Tower Pump - To be able to pump cooling water
- Continuous Level Device - To be able to continuously monitor the level of the tank
- Motor - To be able to convert electrical power into rotary motion
- Starter - To be able to provide electrical power to the motor

Note how each Active Function contains the phrase, "To be able to", and that each function is written at a level that describes its basic function. At this point in the RCM there is no need to describe the performance standard of each support function, this will be discussed when we address the failure modes of each component as they relate to the performance standards of the Main Function.

Passive Function Components
Passive Functions describe the functionality of components which have the potential for hidden failures. These devices are passive by design; they are waiting to recognize a specific condition that will not exist under normal operating conditions for this asset. We describe Passive Function Components by using the phrase, "To be capable of". At this stage of performing your RCM analysis, it is extremely critical to take the time to recognize which components provide Hidden Functions. If we do not identify these components at this point in the RCM, we will likely fail to

identify Hidden Failures that could have catastrophic effects on your business.

Examples of Passive Function Components:

- Emergency Stop Button - To be capable of shutting down the system in the event of an emergency
- High Level Switch - To be capable of shutting down the tank supply and alarming the operator in the event of a high level condition
- Back-Up Cooling Tower Pump - To be capable of pumping cooling tower water in the event the main cooling tower pump fails
- Starter/Overloads - To be capable of disconnecting electrical power in the event of an overload condition

It should be noted at this time that some components will provide more than one function. If the functions are active they can be listed together in one function statement.

Example -
Continuous Flow Meter - To be able to continuously **monitor** and **totalize** water flow

If a component provides more than one function, one being active and the other being passive, these functions should be listed separately.

Example -
Continuous Level Device - To be able to continuously monitor tank level
Continuous Level Device - To be capable of detecting and alarming high level

More on Hidden Functions
I can't stress enough the importance of identifying hidden function components. These components provide critical functionality, and when failed, will not be evident to the operating crew as they perform their normal duties. As I instruct and mentor RCM facilitators, I most often use the e-stop as an example of a Hidden Function Component. As your process operates, the e-stop could be in a failed state and the people operating the equipment, or working around the equipment, would never know the device is in a failed state. The designed intent of the e-stop button is to shut the system down and safely release all potential energy in the event of an emergency. During normal operating conditions, this

device could be failed in a state where, when pressed, the system would not shut down! Think of this device being failed in this state. One of your employees becomes caught in a piece of equipment, someone reacts quickly to press the e-stop and nothing happens! The equipment continues to run and the effects of this failure go from being tragic to catastrophic.

As we list support functions for the components of our assets, facilitators and team members can confuse active and passive functions from time to time. My advice to all facilitators is if you have any question, make the selection that will provide the safest decision. This would always result in treating the component as a passive device. As an example, the most argued device in terms of being considered active or passive is a coupling guard, as we look to write a support function statement we ask the question, "Is the guard active or passive?" Most people reply the guard supports the active function of protecting people from rotating equipment while the equipment is running during normal operating conditions. As an experienced RCM Practitioner, I would offer the argument that the guard is a passive device, while it provides a protective function it is waiting for a specific condition to exist, and the equipment would operate perfectly without the guard. The fail-safe decision in this case is to treat the guard as a passive device.

The other confusion that arises around hidden functions and hidden failures is the amount of time it takes for a failure to become evident.

Some good rules I use to determine if a component is a Hidden Function Component:

- **The component provides a protective function.**
- **The component is waiting to recognize a specific condition.**
- **The component provides a redundant or back up service.**
- **The system will operate perfectly with the item in a failed state.**
- **The functional failure of this item will not be evident to the operating crew as they perform their normal duties.**

Examples of Hidden Function Components:

1. E-Stop
2. Door Safety Switches
3. Equipment Guarding
4. High Level Switches
5. Low Level Switches
6. High Pressure Switches
7. Low Pressure Switches
8. Pressure Relief Valves
9. Rupture Discs
10. Overloads
11. Fuses
12. Vacuum Relief Valves
13. Redundant Components
14. Safety Showers
15. Smoke Detectors
16. Back Up Generators
17. Emergency Lighting
18. High Temperature Switches
19. Low Temperature Switches
20. Any Audible or Visual Alarm
21. Eye Baths
22. Sprinkler Systems
23. Fire Protection/Suppression Systems
24. Air Quality Sensors
25. Volatile Gas/Vapor Detectors
26. Auto Lubricators
27. Battery Back Up Devices
28. Overflows
29. Secondary Containment
30. High Vibration Switches

Functions & Functional Failures
Functional Failures

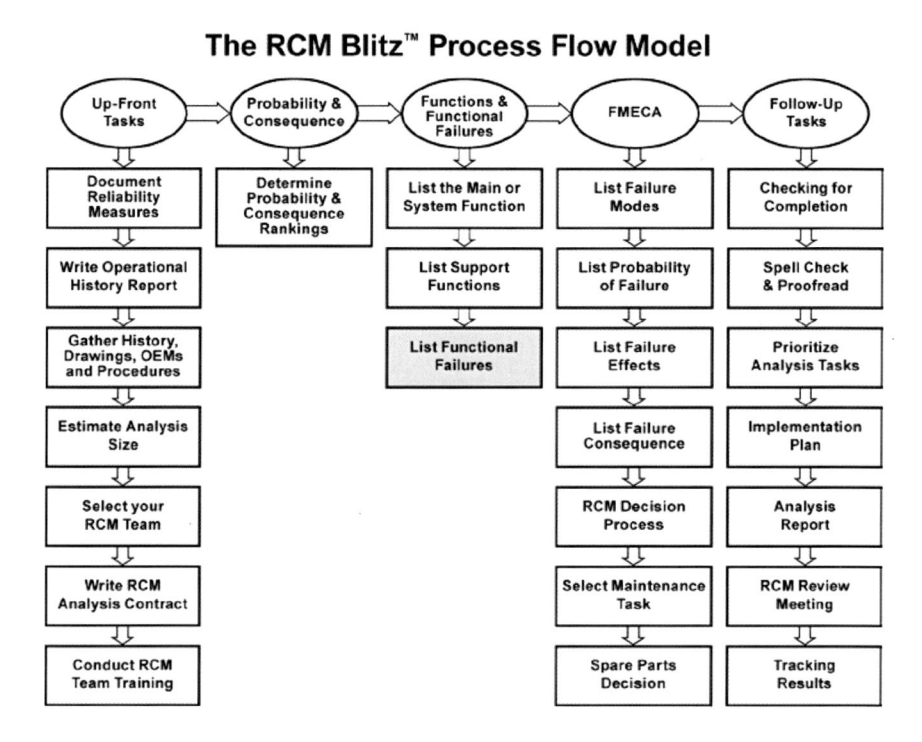

The RCM Blitz™ Process Flow Model

Up-Front Tasks	Probability & Consequence	Functions & Functional Failures	FMECA	Follow-Up Tasks
Document Reliability Measures	Determine Probability & Consequence Rankings	List the Main or System Function	List Failure Modes	Checking for Completion
Write Operational History Report		List Support Functions	List Probability of Failure	Spell Check & Proofread
Gather History, Drawings, OEMs and Procedures		**List Functional Failures**	List Failure Effects	Prioritize Analysis Tasks
Estimate Analysis Size			List Failure Consequence	Implementation Plan
Select your RCM Team			RCM Decision Process	Analysis Report
Write RCM Analysis Contract			Select Maintenance Task	RCM Review Meeting
Conduct RCM Team Training			Spare Parts Decision	Tracking Results

In the twenty-seven years following the release of Nowlan and Heap's Reliability Centered Maintenance, many have struggled to understand the importance of each step in this seven-step reliability tool. Over the years the process has been studied, tested, changed and rearranged as people strive to achieve "world class" levels of reliability with less time and fewer resources. These changes often try to eliminate one or more of the seven steps proven critical in completing a successful effort. In reality, the to key to speed in performing your analyses, while still maintaining a high quality output, is understanding the value in each step of this proven process.

In this section, I will highlight the importance of listing Functional Failures as part of a thorough reliability centered maintenance analysis.

Topics covered will include:

- The definition of a failure and functional failure
- How to write good functional failure statements
- The importance of listing functional failures
- The pitfalls of skipping this critical step in the RCM process

The Definition of Failure and Functional Failure
To truly understand the definition of the term Functional Failure, it is important that your first understand failure. In the past, it was really just failure that defined and warranted the need for maintenance. Most people looked at failure as a black or white term, a component was failed or working, running or shut down. As a result, the world of maintenance in many places became linked to this definition. Maintenance as a group, were the people you called when the equipment was broken. In reality, the definition of failure is very broad and can often be subjective.

Consider the following definitions of the word **Failure:**

Webster's dictionary defines failure as, "*a state of inability to perform a normal function*".

Nowlan and Heap defined failure as, "*an unsatisfactory condition*".

Read these definitions and try to relate them to your equipment or the process you work with. Is it clear to everyone what your "normal functions" are? Does everyone know what a "satisfactory or unsatisfactory condition" is? If we asked everyone who worked with, or operated, this equipment would they all have the same definition of failure, normal functions and unsatisfactory condition? Of course not, and this is what drives us to become more specific in defining failure, as the definition becomes more specific, our ability to clearly understand and pinpoint failure as a group or business increases.

To understand failure, we must first understand the criteria that define failure. These criteria should be set when defining the performance standards for the function of your system (Main Function) and the components that make up the system (Support/Primary Functions). In defining these performance standards, you will clearly define what *failure* is for your process or equipment. In the world of RCM, we use the term *Functional Failure* to help clarify the understanding of what failure is.

Nowlan and Heap defined *functional failure* as, "*the inability of an item (or the equipment containing it) to meet a specified performance standard*".

Now with the understanding that it's functional failure of an item (component or system) that dictates how we define failure, it should be clear to everyone working with, or operating the equipment, when the equipment has failed.

Writing Good Functional Failure Statements
Writing good functional failure statements is clearly dependent on how well your team has defined the functions of your RCM analysis. Some tips to remember as you identify the main and support functions for your equipment:

- Your Main Function statement should be written in a manner that clearly identifies what the equipment is intended for, and all of the performance standards it is expected to maintain, including environmental, health and safety standards.
- Don't rush through the process of writing function statements. It is the function statements that create a roadmap to a complete and thorough RCM analysis.
- Try to identify active and passive functions. This will help to ensure that your team does not miss any hidden function components.

With your function statements complete, you can now begin to identify and list the functional failures for your analysis. As an example, I have listed the main function statement for a chilled water system and its corresponding functional failures.

Chilled Water System Main/Primary Function Statement:
To be able to supply high quality, chilled water at a temperature of 40°F, plus or minus 5°F, at a rate of 120 gallons per minute, while meeting all environmental, health, and safety standards.

Functional Failures of the Chilled Water System

1. *Unable to supply chilled water at all.*
2. *Unable to maintain water temperature above 35°F.*
3. *Unable to maintain water temperature below 45° F.*
4. *Unable to supply water at a rate of 120 gallons per minute.*
5. *Unable to maintain water quality standards.*
6. *Unable to maintain (company, state or government) environmental, health or safety standards.*

The Importance of Listing Functional Failures

With these functional failures now identified, it should be clear to those who operate or maintain the chilled water system, when the system is failed. More importantly, having identified these functional failures, we can begin to discuss the causes for each functional failure. These are known as **Failure Modes**. For each functional failure identified, there are a number of failure modes that could result in that functional failure. Some failure modes will result in total system shut down or being unable to supply water at all, some will result in chilled water flow falling below the required 120 gallons per minute and other failure modes may affect the quality of the chilled water within the system. The importance of identifying and listing functional failures will now become evident within your RCM analysis. In sorting failure modes by functional failure, we begin to create a high-level troubleshooting guide for our process or piece of equipment. When this chilled water system RCM analysis is completed, we will have a complete listing of failure modes that cause each functional failure for both operations and maintenance. Now our equipment operators can begin looking for performance trends. If the temperature of the chilled water were to begin to trend up or down, they will have a compete listing of the failure modes that cause these changes.

The Pitfalls of Skipping Functional Failures

One of the curses of being human is the burning desire to do everything faster. From the time we first learn to walk, we have a desire to run, the minute the first automobiles hit the road, someone had to make a faster one. In the world of manufacturing and maintenance, speed can be a good thing but it can also be a bad thing. From the time Nowlan and Heap first designed and implemented RCM, people have been in search of ways to make it faster, and in most cases they do so by eliminating some of the key process steps. In many cases, functions and functional failures are steps that are eliminated or partly eliminated. In each case, the result is an incomplete RCM analysis and an incomplete maintenance strategy. The well-meaning attempt to save time is usually driven by an inexperienced facilitator, who does not have a full understanding of the consequences, or an impatient manager, with even less understanding. The list below outlines consequences of skipping functions and/or functional failures when performing RCM.

Skipping Functions, Listing Only a Main Function, or Skipping Functional Failures results in:

- **Incomplete listing of failure modes** - *How can one expect a complete listing of failures without identifying each component?*

- **Incomplete listing of hidden failures** - *If we don't discuss each component, and its intended function, would we expect to discover failures that are not evident?*

- **The inability to recognize when a functional failure has occurred** - *Failure to recognize functional failure is key in beginning to recognize and understand potential failures and the P-F Curve.*

- **Improper applications of Preventive Maintenance and On-Condition Maintenance** - *Functions, Performance Standards and Functional Failures are all key components in understanding the use of on-condition maintenance and predictive technologies. Failure to identify these key components often results in preventive maintenance being applied where on-condition maintenance would be more applicable and effective.*

- **An incomplete and therefore less effective maintenance strategy** - *With all of the above being true, how would one expect an effective maintenance strategy as a finished product?*

In closing, when correctly applied, Reliability Centered Maintenance has a long and successful history as the best process for building a complete and effective maintenance strategy. This success can be easily replicated and achieved through learning the RCM process and sharing our experiences (*successes and failures*). As RCM practitioners, we also understand that improvement to the process can only come as a result of change to the process, and this requires that steps be either added or eliminated. My advice, if you're thinking about eliminating a step, would be to get on the phone, or go on the internet, and contact a few RCM practitioners to talk about the elimination. Chances are most of us have tried it. If you're looking to add a step for improvement, try it out, see if it works and adds value. If it does, keep it to yourself, you may have a new methodology!

CHAPTER 5
FMECA

Failure Modes and Probability of Failure

The RCM Blitz™ Process Flow Model

```
Up-Front Tasks → Probability & Consequence → Functions & Functional Failures → FMECA → Follow-Up Tasks
```

Up-Front Tasks	Probability & Consequence	Functions & Functional Failures	FMECA	Follow-Up Tasks
Document Reliability Measures	Determine Probability & Consequence Rankings	List the Main or System Function	**List Failure Modes**	Checking for Completion
Write Operational History Report		List Support Functions	**List Probability of Failure**	Spell Check & Proofread
Gather History, Drawings, OEMs and Procedures		List Functional Failures	List Failure Effects	Prioritize Analysis Tasks
Estimate Analysis Size			List Failure Consequence	Implementation Plan
Select your RCM Team			RCM Decision Process	Analysis Report
Write RCM Analysis Contract			Select Maintenance Task	RCM Review Meeting
Conduct RCM Team Training			Spare Parts Decision	Tracking Results

Reliability Centered Maintenance is a structured reliability tool designed to create a complete maintenance strategy for a process or piece of equipment. Developed in the 1970's by United Airlines employees, Stan Nowlan and Howard Heap, the process has since been crafted into several RCM variations and methodologies, each using slightly different paths to reach a final task outcome designed to mitigate the consequences of a given failure mode.

While each methodology may differ slightly, they all at some point in the process address failure modes, the specific manner of failure, and the circumstances or sequence of events which lead to functional failure.

While the concept of identifying why your process has failed may seem simple, this is one of the big stumbling blocks of Reliability Centered Maintenance. Correctly identifying failure modes is highly critical to the overall success of your RCM analysis. If your Failure Modes are not written at the correct level, and fail to identify the specific cause of failure, your team may also fail to identify the correct maintenance task for mitigating the failure.

To help to first understand proper Failure Mode identification I will first offer a three part formula that I use to help teams in this stage of the process. Every failure mode should include the following three components: Part + Problem + Specific Cause of Failure = Failure Mode

   a. The definition of "part" is a group of pieces that make up a component.
      i. Examples from ISO standard: impeller, seal, shaft, bolt, nut, bearing
   b. The definition of "Problem" is the effect of the failure mechanism
      i. Examples: failed, damaged, out of adjustment, seized, fatigued, burnt, broken
   c. The definition of "Specific Cause" is the physical cause of the problem
      i. Examples: age, improper lubrication, misalignment, imbalance, improper installation

Example:

Cooling Water Pump Bearing (Part) seizes (Problem) due to lack of lubrication (Specific Cause of Failure)

Having now identified a proper failure mode, the team can move on to describe the failure effects and consequences and make a sound decision on how to best mitigate this specific failure mode. Looking at the failure mode identified above, can you venture a guess at what the task might be?

Was your answer to develop a lubrication task that identifies the correct type, amount and interval of lubrication? We set that task up as part of our maintenance strategy and we have now ensured that this failure mode is not likely to ever occur.

Common Mistakes in Writing Failure Modes
While this three part formula may seem simple, I can offer many examples of how people fall down when it comes to writing failure modes.

Writing Failure Modes at a level too high to make sound decisions
Using the acetone unload pump as an example, what would happen if I decided to make my RCM analysis go faster by writing the failure mode - **The cooling water pump fails.** What task should I implement to mitigate this failure mode? Dropping a step closer to actual failure mode I could also write - **The cooling water pump bearing fails.**

Looking at that failure mode, are we any closer to understanding why the bearing failed and as a result could we develop a sound maintenance task? We might elect to perform vibration analysis to detect the bearing is in the process of failing. The question is, do we want to use vibration analysis to inform us that someone forgot to lubricate the pump bearing?

Combining/Grouping Failure Modes
The second most common mistake is combining or grouping failure modes. Looking back again on the failure mode - **Cooling water pump bearing fails due to lack of lubrication.** What would happen if I made the decision to write the failure mode as - **Cooling water pump bearing fails due to improper lubrication**?

In making the decision to group the individual lubrication failure modes can I now expect the team to come up with a sound task? How many individual failure modes are now grouped into this one statement? The list below is a partial look at what might be included in the failure mode grouping of improper lubrication:

1. Cooling water pump bearing fails due to lack of lubrication.
2. Cooling water pump bearing fails due to incorrect type of lubrication.
3. Cooling water pump bearing fails due to contaminated lubrication.
4. Cooling water pump bearing fails due to over-lubrication.
5. Cooling water pump bearing fails due to lubrication breakdown.

Using Failure Modes Lists
While failure modes lists can be helpful and can speed up the RCM process, the lists often create more problems than they solve. The overall objective of a RCM analysis should be more than listing the known failure modes of the components that make up the system you're

analyzing. The discussion and discovery of the likely failure modes in your plant is an educational tool for your facilitators and team members. It opens discussion to build an understanding of the failures that have, and could occur, at your plant. In visiting manufacturing plants around the world, those with the worst equipment reliability have the highest levels of reactive maintenance. As we begin to perform RCM analyses at these sites, we see one glaring problem, their reactive maintenance culture has morphed their maintenance personnel into component replacers instead of equipment maintainers. As a result, when asked to begin failure mode identification they rarely know or understand the specific causes of failures.

The problem with failure modes lists:

1. Most lists are not complete, I thought this until I saw one that had 168 failure modes for a ball valve. So while most are not complete, I have yet to find one that will address YOUR failure modes.
2. They dumb down the learning process of failure mode identification.
3. They slow the learning/certification process for RCM facilitators.
4. They often result in discussion/consideration of failure modes that are highly unlikely at your plant.

Overuse of the "Black Box" failure mode

The term "Black Box" in RCM comes from airline industry flight data recorders. In the world of RCM, we use the term to describe the chunking of several failure modes into a two-part failure mode, "The component fails."

The excuse to black box typically comes into play for two reasons:

1. We don't know how the component works.
2. Regardless of the cause, the failure effect is identical for all its failure modes.

I offer the sound advice that if we don't know how it works, now is a good time to learn. The second excuse is normally used as a team pushes to complete a given RCM analysis. As the week goes on, there is a tendency to rush the process. At this point, I urge teams to list and discuss the failure modes and tasks as we often miss significant improvement opportunities when pressed to complete.

While I caution facilitators to not black box failure modes, there are times when it is an acceptable process. These rare situations are listed below under exceptions to the 3-Part Failure Mode Formula.

Exceptions to the 3-Part Failure Mode Formula
The craft of writing good failure modes comes through a thorough understanding of the following three items:

1. The Six Conditional Probability of Failure Curves
2. The Potential Failure Curve (P-F Curve)
3. The Specific Causes of Failure for Equipment Components

There are failure modes that occur at your plant that do not, and will not, fit the 3-Part formula. These exceptions typically come in the form of low-voltage, solid-state electronic components that have a random conditional probability of failure, as well as a very short (part of a second) potential failure interval.

Example: Palletizer Product Jam Proximity Switch Fails Electrically Open - The product jam proximity switch is a solid state, low voltage component and is subject to random electronic failures (*Failure Pattern - F*). When the device fails, there is little or no sign of potential failure and it very quickly (within a fraction of a second) has functionally failed. For this failure, there is no specific cause, just a location (Palletizer) and a component (Proximity Switch).

Failure Patterns: 1960s & 1970s Data

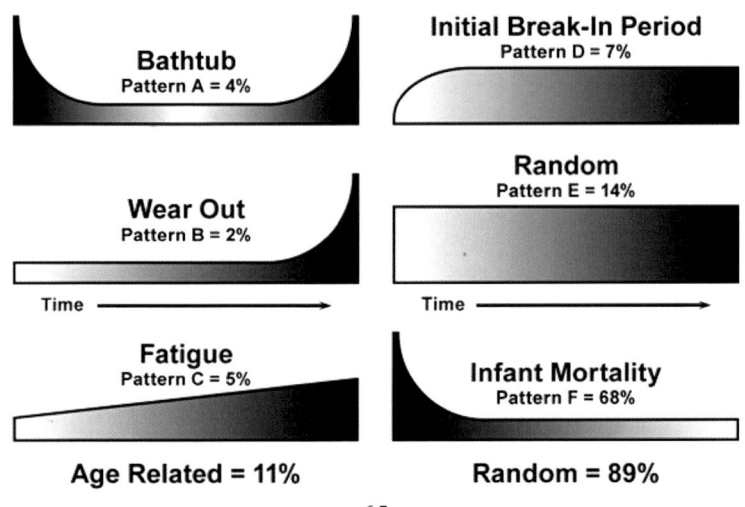

Bathtub — Pattern A = 4%
Wear Out — Pattern B = 2%
Fatigue — Pattern C = 5%

Age Related = 11%

Initial Break-In Period — Pattern D = 7%
Random — Pattern E = 14%
Infant Mortality — Pattern F = 68%

Random = 89%

It is often with these types of components that facilitators and teams become tempted to group, or black box, failure modes, using a failure mode that might read:

1. Palletizer Product Jam Proximity Switch Fails.

The logic being that if the Palletizer Product Jam switch fails to cycle open and close at least once every 30 seconds, the conveyor will stop, and the operator will receive a Palletizer Conveyor Product Jam Alarm.

The danger, in this logic of grouping, is we have missed the following valid failure modes:

1. Palletizer Product Jam Proximity Switch fails open due to improper adjustment.
2. Palletizer Product Jam Proximity Switch fails open due to physical damage.
3. Palletizer Product Jam Proximity Switch fails open due to water contamination.
4. Palletizer Product Jam Proximity Switch fails open due to being dirty.

Remember to perform your analysis and write your failure modes at the level in which you maintain each component.
Reliability Centered Maintenance becomes very painful when we begin writing failure modes to a detail we no longer repair at. I often use the example of a ½ inch ball valve. Regardless of what the valve is supplying or isolating, if it fails in any way (open, closed, leaking internally or externally) what will you do with this valve? Throw it out, and replace it with a new ½ inch ball valve. As a result, we can simply write the failure mode as:

- Acetone supply pump ½ inch sample valve fails open, or
- Acetone supply pump ½ inch sample valve fails closed.

This is a good example of a two-part failure mode.

While it is nice to be able to write component failure modes at the level you maintain them, you must also be careful not to miss the possibility of mitigating a dominant failure mode. Let's say for example, we are about to assess a 1-horse power electric motor. When this motor fails, we will throw out the failed motor and replace it with a new motor. The temptation here is to write the failure mode, "Product conveyor drive motor fails", assess the failure effects and jump to the typical, "No Scheduled Maintenance" task. While at this point I have no problem with the failure mode, as the motor is a "throw away" item, I do insist the facilitators follow the RCM process and be sure to assess the frequency at which this motor fails. If the motor has never failed, or let's say, has failed one time in ten years, the no scheduled maintenance decision would be correct. But, consider what you would do if the team informed you that this motor fails once a month or more? Would running the component to failure be your best strategy? The answer of course is no. Always remember to consider the frequency at which throw-away items fail, and if this frequency is too high, pull the team back and assess the specific failure modes for the component.

When to Black Box
When it comes to writing a high level failure mode, or black box failure mode, only write a high level failure mode for a component that is critical to your system but is not within the boundaries of your RCM analysis. For instance, your RCM team is performing an analysis on a large equipment drive unit that has a hydraulic brake. The drive unit alone has more than enough components for a full RCM analysis and the Hydraulic system also has enough components to be a stand alone RCM. In performing the RCM analysis on the drive system, you might write one failure mode for the hydraulic brake - *Drive system hydraulic brake fails* - and as task for this failure mode you would write - *Perform RCM analysis on drive system hydraulic brake.*

Confusing Failure Modes and Failure Effects
Reliability Centered Maintenance is all about understanding the relationship between cause and effect. Seasoned RCM and RCA facilitators often bring their greatest value by helping team participants understand this relationship and identify tasks to mitigate the effects of a failure, instead of the cause.

I once worked with a company on a closed loop conveyance system that suffered weekly four-hour shutdowns to replace the absolute filter prior to the main compressor. The operations and maintenance group were proud of the fact that they had developed an on-condition task that alarmed high differential pressure across the filter. This gave them time to get the filter and gaskets from the stockroom, and cut the downtime from 6 to 4 hours. As we began discussing the absolute filter as a component, the team quickly identified, "Conveyance system absolute filter plugs due to normal use". I asked the team, "Why is the filter plugging on a weekly basis and is that really normal?" After some discussion, we determined that the filter was plugging with product carried over from the dust collector. I then asked the question, "What level of filtration should the dust collector provide?"

In the end, we determined the tube sheet gasket in the dust collector was leaking, allowing product to plug the absolute filter. Upon completing this one-time task to replace the gasket, the absolute filter remained in place for over two years without plugging. By eliminating the cause of the dust leak, we eliminated the effect of the filter plugging.

To a seasoned RCM facilitator, it's easy to spot failure modes that contain failure effects, they often contain the word "fails" more than once or the words "because, or as a result of".

Examples:

- Cooling Water Pump impeller fails due to cavitation because the suction valve was left closed - In this case, the pump impeller cavitation is a failure effect of the failure mode: Acetone pump suction valve fails closed due to instrument air hose leak.

- Palletizer drive gearbox fails due to over temperature condition caused by lack of lubrication - The failure mode here should read: Palletizer gearbox fails due to lack of lubrication. Over heating of the gearbox is a failure effect of not having enough lubrication.

- Palletizer Product Jam Limit Switch fails open due to improper adjustment due to the mounting bracket being loose - The failure mode should be: Palletizer product jam limit switch mounting bracket is loose due to improper installation. The mounting bracket being improperly installed results in the proximity switch being unable to detect product.

The Danger of Writing Failure Effects as Failure Modes
This problem/concept might be the most difficult to identify and understand as a new RCM facilitator. It's also one of the reasons I encourage people to participate in the RCM facilitator mentoring and certification process. The identification of the correct specific cause for each failure mode, and the assessment of that cause, is what leads the team to identify the correct maintenance task.

The problem with having a failure effect written as a failure mode is that the team is now attempting to select a task to mitigate the effect of the failure, instead of the cause, and as a result, they are not likely to reduce or eliminate the actual failure.

List the Probability of Failure
After each failure mode has been listed and entered in the RCM database we will need to determine the probability of each failure by referring to the probability and consequence statements developed with the RCM team prior to the start of the analysis.

FMECA
Failure Effects and Consequences

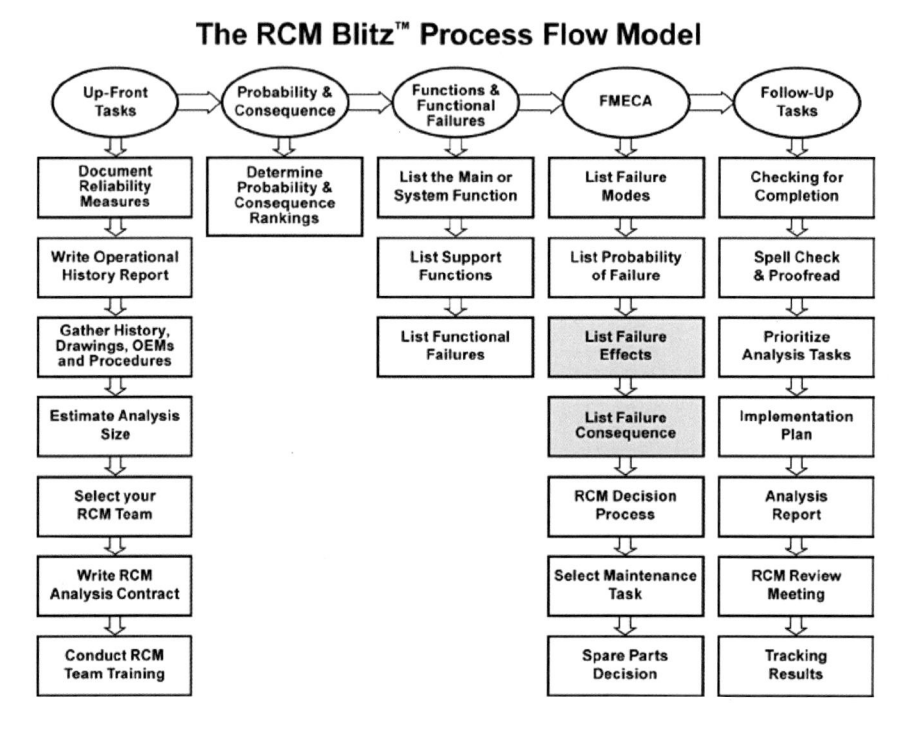

The RCM Blitz™ Process Flow Model

```
Up-Front Tasks → Probability & Consequence → Functions & Functional Failures → FMECA → Follow-Up Tasks
```

Up-Front Tasks	Probability & Consequence	Functions & Functional Failures	FMECA	Follow-Up Tasks
Document Reliability Measures	Determine Probability & Consequence Rankings	List the Main or System Function	List Failure Modes	Checking for Completion
Write Operational History Report		List Support Functions	List Probability of Failure	Spell Check & Proofread
Gather History, Drawings, OEMs and Procedures		List Functional Failures	List Failure Effects	Prioritize Analysis Tasks
Estimate Analysis Size			List Failure Consequence	Implementation Plan
Select your RCM Team			RCM Decision Process	Analysis Report
Write RCM Analysis Contract			Select Maintenance Task	RCM Review Meeting
Conduct RCM Team Training			Spare Parts Decision	Tracking Results

When I first began learning about, and performing RCM analyses, for Eastman Kodak Company in the 1990's, I was always tempted as a facilitator to rush through the failure effects step of RCM. The failure effect describes what happened to the asset and why we care that this specific failure mode has occurred. While this process of writing failure effects seemed simple to me, it was like pulling teeth to get my RCM teams to participate in the process. In most cases, while I knew what I wanted the team to list as failure effects, I did not fully understand the context in which they operated their equipment, nor the true effects, signals, or alarms, associated with each failure mode.

The one hard and fast rule that I focus on when writing failure effect statements is that the statement must contain enough information necessary for the team to easily assess the consequence of each failure mode. To achieve this rule I have created the following minimal requirements for failure effect statements.

Failure Effect Statement Requirements:

1. Events that lead up to failure or functional failure
2. First sign of evidence
3. Secondary effects/damage
4. Effects that impact product quality
5. Effects that could result in health, safety or environmental incidents and accidents
6. Events required to bring the process back to normal operating condition

Understanding the Requirements

Listing failure effect statements can seem a bit slow and punishing at times. The trick here is to understand the value in fulfilling each of the requirements. For each requirement, there is a specific reason why the RCM team needs to take the time to consider and write each requirement for the failure effect statement. To make this clear, I will list each requirement, describe what it takes to fulfill the requirement, describe why we need this information and also make clear the danger of not considering or including each step.

Events Leading Up to the Failure

Part one of the failure effects statement should help the RCM team to understand if the failure mode falls under one of the three wear-based failure curves or the three random-based failure curves. Events leading up to the failure should clearly describe the effects of wear-based failure with statements that describe what occurs as the component wears.

Example - If the failure mode we are assessing is, "Fuel piping leaks due to corrosion", we want the team to describe what happens to the component (piping) as it corrodes. The failure effect statement should start with the phrase, "Corrosion of the fuel pipe results in thinning of the pipe walls". This description clearly tells what the failure mode is (corrosion) and possible evidence of what is occurring to the component as the failure progresses along the potential failure curve.

Wear-based failure modes that fit conditional probability of failure curves A, B, and C should always have events that lead to failure. Things like corrosion, erosion, abrasion, and normal wear.

Random-based failures can be a bit trickier to understand as some do give off signs of evidence with a useful P-F interval while other random failures happen immediately with limited, or no, evidence of failure.

Example - The failure mode we are assessing is, "Product jam proximity switch fails open". The opening failure effect statement for this failure mode would be, "In the event the product jam proximity switch fails open". The statement "In the event," indicates the failure mode happens very quickly and is random in nature. When this component fails, it provides little or no evidence that the failure is about to occur.

The value in having the RCM team consider events leading up to the failure is that they should now understand if the failure mode is random or wear based. This clear understanding will also help the team to assign a task using the RCM decision process.

First Sign of Evidence
Part two of the RCM failure effects requirements is the first sign of evidence. The first sign of evidence requirement forces the RCM team to consider how each specific failure mode becomes evident to the operating crew as they perform their normal duties. In other words, what notifies the operators that a failure has occurred?

If we look at the first failure mode, "Fuel Piping leaks due to corrosion", to fulfill the requirements for first sign of evidence, we need to enter into the failure effect statement how the operators, or people who work at this plant, will first recognize that the corrosion of the pipe has resulted in a fuel leak.

Depending on the plant, how they operate the asset, as well as the presence of back up protective devices, affects the way the failure first becomes evident. Consider the different ways this failure could become evident:

Plant 1 has an internal tank pump, all its fuel piping installed above ground and has installed fuel vapor detectors at three strategic locations between the fuel tank and the load out truck. Should the vapor detectors detect the presence of fuel vapors there will be an audible alarm and the system will shut down.

Plant 2 has an internal tank pump and all its piping is installed underground between the fuel tank and load out truck. Fuel leaks are detected by taking inventory each week and looking for discrepancies between what was delivered to the fuel tank and what was loaded out to the trucks.

Plant 3 has an internal tank pump and its piping is installed above ground between the tank and load out truck. There are no fuel vapor detectors but the operators are required to inspect the fuel piping for leaks each time they load out a truck.

Looking at these three examples, we now see three different ways that the same failure mode can become evident, as well as three, quite drastic, differences in how long it takes for the failure mode to become evident. Some might even say that the failure at plant 2 is not evident, it's hidden, asking the question, "How long would it take to recognize this failure?" It is questions like these that clearly point out the danger of not discussing evidence as part of your failure effect statements. Here the failure is always evident, but the time it takes to reveal itself is longer at plants 1 and 3, and when the leak at plant 2 becomes large enough, it will become very evident.

We can not close the discussion of first sign of evidence without discussing hidden failure modes. Hidden failure modes result from the functional failure of a component that is not evident to the operating crew under performance of their normal duties. As your plant runs in normal operating condition the failure of these devices will not be evident. The process will, in fact, run on perfectly as if nothing has occurred. The two failure modes listed here are hidden failure modes:

1. Fuel system emergency stop button is failed closed - This e-stop button is wired normally closed. Should it fail in the closed state during normal operating conditions, the process would continue to run as if nothing has occurred. The only way this failure will become evident is if something else happens, or occurs, to make the failure evident. Example - The operator notices a gasket leak and presses the e-stop button to stop the process, with the button failed in the closed state the process will not shut down but the operator now knows the button has failed.
2. Back up fuel pump motor is failed due to lack of lubrication - The key part of this failure mode are the words "back up", this should indicate that the failure mode for the pump specified is on a back up system. During normal operating conditions, the primary or main fuel pump is used to transfer fuel from the fuel tank to the load out truck. The failure of a back up device is not evident during normal operating conditions. The only way this failure mode will become evident is if some part of the primary or main pump system fails requiring the start up of the back up system.

Secondary Effects or Damage

The third failure effects requirement deals with secondary effects or damages that result from the failure mode that the team is assessing. It is in this portion of the failure effect statement that we begin to discuss what happens when the failure becomes evident, and the possible extent of the damage to our business. It is important to understand that at this point we discuss each failure as if nothing is being done to prevent or stop the failure from occurring. This portion of the failure effect statement often uses the phrase, "if left to its own devices" or "if left to fail".

The importance of discussing secondary effects or damage allows the team to understand the potential consequences at risk if we ignore each specific failure. One of the most underestimated benefits of performing an RCM analysis and implementing the tasks is that a fully implemented RCM will provide a maintenance strategy that will ensure the inherent designed reliability of the asset at a minimum cost. The key phrase here is "minimum cost". The cost of maintenance for companies who fail to understand the value of reliability is astronomically higher than the cost for companies who do. The difference in cost comes from performing maintenance in a fire-fighting mode. Emergency and demand maintenance costs are typically 3 to 5 times higher than planned and scheduled maintenance and one of the big reasons is secondary equipment damage.

Imagine if you are driving down the road in your car and suddenly you notice the oil pressure light comes on. You now have a decision to make, you can ignore the light and drive on (after all you do have some important things to do) or you can find a safe place to pull over to investigate why the light came on. With just this information, which decision would you make?

I have been asking this question for years, when instructing facilitators and leading RCM teams through the analysis process, and I have yet to have one person say, "Drive on, it's just an alarm". Yet, while at work, we continue to ignore similar alarms on a daily basis. I then follow-up with the question, "Why would you stop your car to investigate the cause of the low oil pressure light?" Again I get the consistent answer, "Your engine oil could be low or leaking and you might seize your engine. That would cost you a lot of money". The cost of stopping, determining the cause of the light and making the repair, would be far less than the cost of ignoring the alarm and allowing the engine to seize. The exact same scenario occurs day to day in manufacturing equipment, yet, in many cases, we make the choice to ignore various alarms. The resulting secondary damage drives up the cost of maintenance, as well as the time the equipment is down for repair.

Product Quality Effects
In the past five years, I have performed RCM analyses for two major companies who made the request that we not consider product quality as part of the RCM process (for obvious reasons they shall remain nameless). Their reasoning was that Quality is a separate organization in their business and it is their job to deal with product quality issues. Maintenance on the other hand is charged with equipment reliability, they need only be concerned with keeping the equipment running. Needless to say, I found this to be a disturbing business concept. If your equipment is running but making mountains of rejected product, do you consider this process to be reliable? Of course not! As we look at the reliability measures of OEE and TEEP, quality is identified as one of the key manufacturing loss categories. We should also understand that maintenance provides a key role in terms of eliminating, or reducing, the occurrence of failure modes that result in off spec product.

As we discuss failure effects, we should always take into account if the failure mode will, in any way, affect product quality. Should this be the case, we identify the potential effects in the failure effect statement.

For example, in discussing the failure mode of "worn wear strips" on the side of the Callahan Brewing beer conveyor, in the failure effects statement we would mention that if left to their own devices, the wear strips could wear to a point where the beer cases come in contact with the wear strip hardware resulting in damaged cases. Again, if we ignore the failure, the resulting consequences will impact the quality of our product and a simple maintenance task could completely eliminate the failure.

Health, Safety and Environmental Effects
Health, Safety and Environmental effects are the resulting consequences for failure modes that result from a loss of function that could affect HSE. It is important to note that as we list failure effects and make RCM decisions, we will always default to the best fail-safe decision. This is why we ask the question in the RCM Blitz™ decision diagram using "could" instead of "will". The fail-safe decision ensures we do not make a decision to run to failure when failure modes impact HSE.

As we identify these effects during the analysis process, we will want to clearly state the possible hazards and impact to our people, customers and business if the failure is ignored.

Looking at the failure of the Callahan Brewing conveyor e-stop switch in a closed condition, we would write - **In the event the beer conveyor e-stop were to fail in a closed condition, it would not shut down the system when pressed. This failure could result in serious injury to personnel.**

Events Required to Bring Functions Back to Normal Operating Condition
This is the easiest step in listing failure effect statements. We simply list what we want our operator to do should this failure occur. In most cases we enter the phrase - The operator will shut down the equipment and contact maintenance to troubleshoot and repair. There are, however, cases where the resulting phrase would be different. For example, if we were discussing the failure of a pumping system that had primary and back up pumps that did not activate automatically on failure, we would say the operator would lock out the primary pump and start the back up.

Finishing Out Failure Effects
As we finish completing the failure effect statements, the RCM facilitator will now ask two quick questions to complete the effects information.

1. What is the frequency of this failure mode?
2. How much down time will result from this failure mode?

The question of frequency addresses the estimated occurrence of this specific failure mode, for the component we are discussing, pertaining only to the asset we are performing the analysis on. This information is used to remind the RCM team how often this failure is experienced prior to making task decisions.

The question of down time delivers a key piece of information for consequence decisions that are not HSE related. Knowing the equipment down time informs the team of the operational consequences of each specific failure mode.

As a RCM facilitator, I typically direct this question to the equipment operators as they have the best perspective of what down time is. To best represent what we are looking for I have developed the following chart:

What Is Downtime?
- Equipment Fails
- Operator Troubleshoots
- Operator Contacts Maintenance
- Maintenance Responds
- Maintenance Troubleshoots
- Lock Out Tag Out Try Out
- Locate Parts Needed
- Order Parts Needed
- Make Repair
- Return LOTOTO
- Restart

List the Consequence of Failure

Once you have facilitated the team through the failure effects statements, they can now determine the consequence of this failure by referring back to the consequence statements developed prior to the start of the analysis.

FMECA
RCM Decision Process

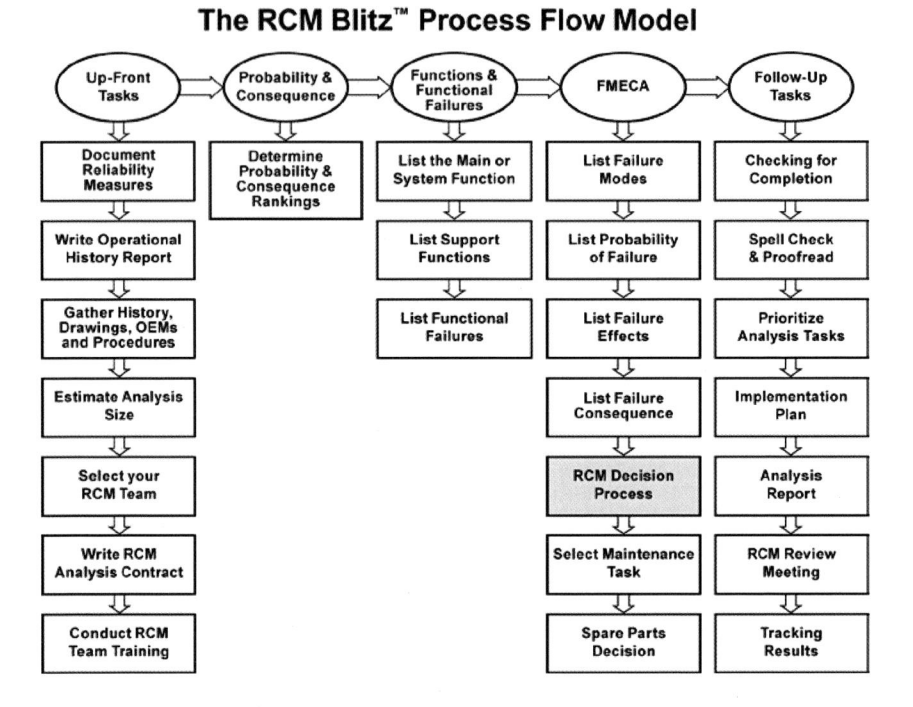

The RCM Blitz™ Process Flow Model

Up-Front Tasks
- Document Reliability Measures
- Write Operational History Report
- Gather History, Drawings, OEMs and Procedures
- Estimate Analysis Size
- Select your RCM Team
- Write RCM Analysis Contract
- Conduct RCM Team Training

Probability & Consequence
- Determine Probability & Consequence Rankings

Functions & Functional Failures
- List the Main or System Function
- List Support Functions
- List Functional Failures

FMECA
- List Failure Modes
- List Probability of Failure
- List Failure Effects
- List Failure Consequence
- **RCM Decision Process**
- Select Maintenance Task
- Spare Parts Decision

Follow-Up Tasks
- Checking for Completion
- Spell Check & Proofread
- Prioritize Analysis Tasks
- Implementation Plan
- Analysis Report
- RCM Review Meeting
- Tracking Results

The RCM Blitz™ Decision Diagram

The RCM Blitz™ decision diagram is a flow diagram used to lead the RCM team to the best decision for mitigating the consequences for each failure mode addressed in the RCM analysis.

The first question in the decision process is, "Will the failure be detected by the operating crew as they perform their normal duties?"

While this question may sound simple enough, it often needs to be explained. We need to determine if this failure is hidden or evident.

When we look at the word failure, we are really discussing functional failure.

Allied Reliability - RCM Blitz
Reliability Centered Maintenance Decision Flow Chart

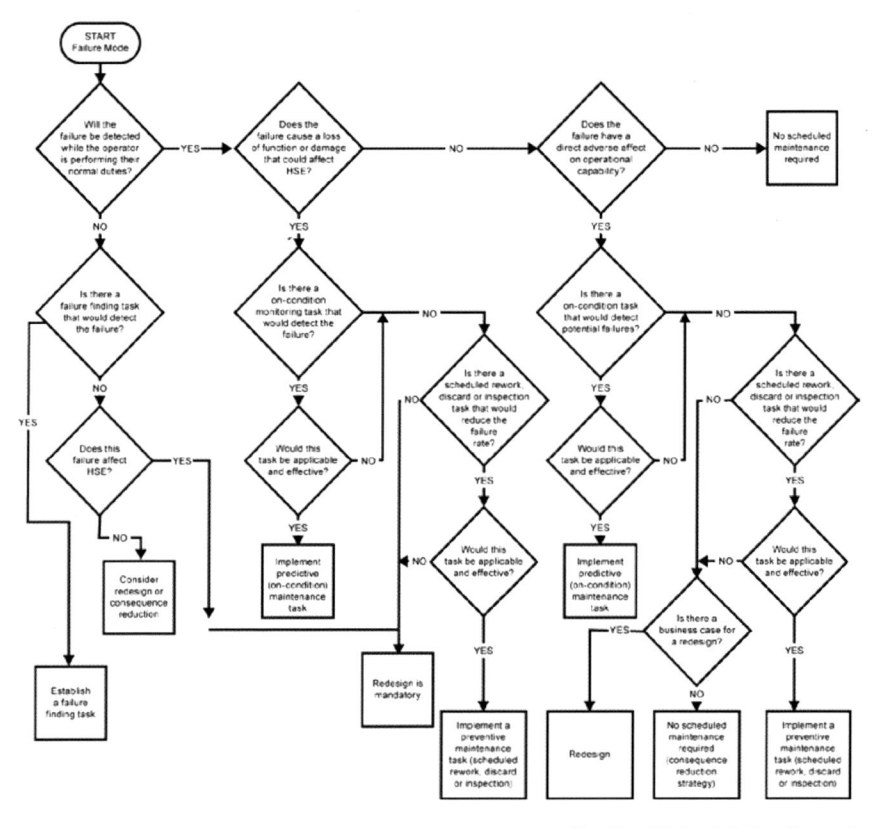

(See Pg. 125 for full-size diagram)

If we were discussing the failure mode of a bearing (seizing due to misalignment) many operators would never know that it was a bearing that had seized, let alone what caused the failure. (When we refer to the operating crew in this question, it is anyone who works with, or around, this equipment. It could be an equipment operator, a maintenance mechanic, an engineer or a manager.) However, when the bearing seizes, the motor overloads and shuts down and the operator gets a motor overload alarm. The process has stopped and there was an alarm, both of these things are evident.

So when is a failure not evident?

Hidden failures are not evident. They allow your equipment to run perfectly, during normal operating conditions, when the hidden function component is in a failed state. For example, if you have an emergency stop button on your equipment, the E-Stop could be failed in a state where if pressed to stop the machine, nothing happens. The machine would continue to run because the E-Stop is in a failed state, but it was not evident.

Once the RCM team has made the decision that a failure is not evident, the diagram then leads to the question, "Is there a failure-finding task that would detect the failure?"

The question is referring to a (failure finding) task that can be done, on a scheduled basis, to detect failures that have already occurred but are not evident to the operating crew. Is there any way to test the functionality of this device, on a schedule, to see if it still works properly?

Answering yes to the failure finding task leads to the question, "Is this task applicable and effective[1]?" This is the most common question in the RCM Blitz™ decision diagram. The intent of the "applicable and effective" question is to ensure your team is selecting the best task to mitigate the failure mode being discussed.

In terms of failure-finding tasks, applicable and effective mean the following:

Applicable - The task selected will clearly detect the component is in a failed state.

Effective - The task selected is cost effective and will produce a consistent result using a concise job plan.

Answering yes to the applicable/effective question results in implementing the failure finding task. Answering no leads you to the last question in the hidden failure leg of the decision tree, "Does the failure

---

[1] Derek Burley is a Reliability Manager at Rio Tinto in Salt Lake City and has been a RCM Practitioner for 15 years. Derek provided assistance in writing the section on RCM Blitz decisions specific to what makes each task Applicable or Effective.

impact health, safety or environment?" Answering yes to this question leads to mandatory redesign, making it clear that any hidden failure that affects HSE, and cannot be addressed through a failure finding task, must be resolved through redesign.

Health Safety and Environmental Decisions
Going back to the start of the decision diagram, we begin to address each failure mode with the question, "Will the failure be detected by the operating crew as they perform their normal duties?" Answering yes to this question leads us to the first question in the HSE leg of the decision diagram, "Does the failure cause a loss of function that could affect health, safety or environment?"

Going into some detail on this question, I have some hard and fast rules when it comes to HSE failure modes:

1. I never argue about the word could, if someone on the team says the failure mode could have HSE consequences, we will go down the HSE leg of the decision tree.

2. I never allow the RCM team to set standards to define HSE. A spill is a spill, whether it is 1 drop or 1,000 gallons. A specific safety hazard could be a near miss one day and the next day it could blind someone. Addressing failure modes in the HSE leg of the decision diagram is the fail safe way to address potential problems.

Answering yes to the question, "Does the failure cause a loss of function that could affect health, safety or environment?" leads to the question, "Is there an on condition task that would detect potential failure?"

In order to answer yes to this question and have the task be both applicable and effective, the task must be able to detect a specific condition (i.e. vibration) with an explicit task (i.e. vibration analysis) at a reasonably consistent P-F interval. This task must also reduce the risk of failure to a tolerable level and be cost effective.

If there is not an applicable or effective on-condition task, we then ask the question, "Is there a scheduled rework, discard or inspection task that would reduce the failure rate?"

In order to answer yes to the PM task, an applicable mitigating task must identify a consistent age at which the conditional probability of failure rapidly increases and that ALL failures occur after this age. To be effective, the task must reduce the rate of failure to a tolerable level and be cost effective in doing so.

In the event the team does not select an on-condition or PM task, the decision process now leads to the statement that redesign is mandatory. The failure mode must be eliminated.

Operational Decisions

Should the RCM team answer no to the question regarding health, safety or environment, the diagram then leads to the operational leg of the decision tree asking the question, "Does the failure have a direct adverse affect on operational capability?"

The operational leg of the decision tree asks a series of questions designed to mitigate failure modes that affect the scheduled operating use of the equipment. Every failure mode that costs money has an impact on operational consequences.

I include the following as operational consequences:

1. Cost of lost production
2. Cost of waste
3. Cost of replacement parts
4. Cost of maintenance
5. Inefficient use of operating equipment (Energy waste)

Answering yes to the operational consequence question leads again to the question, "Is there an on-condition task that would detect potential failures?" In order for the on-condition task to be considered applicable and effective it must be able to detect a specific condition (i.e. vibration) with an explicit task (i.e. vibration analysis) at a reasonably consistent P-F interval. This task must also reduce the risk of failure to a tolerable level and be cost effective.

If there is not an applicable or effective on-condition task, we then ask the question, "Is there a scheduled rework, discard or inspection task that would reduce the failure rate?"

In order to answer yes to the PM task, an applicable mitigating task must identify a consistent age at which the conditional probability of failure rapidly increases and that only a tolerable number of failures occur after this age. To be effective the task must reduce the rate of failure to a tolerable level and be cost effective in doing so.

In the event there is not an applicable or effective on-condition or PM task, the diagram then asks the question, "Is there a business case for redesign?"

In order for a redesign to be considered applicable or effective it must do one of the following:

1. Reduce the conditional probability of failure to an acceptable level - and/or
2. Eliminate the failure - and/or
3. Change the failure of this item from hidden to evident

In the event there is not a business case for redesign, the decision diagram then leads to a, "No scheduled maintenance required, consequence reduction task" decision. I am a firm believer that no failure mode should ever lead to making a decision to do nothing in regards to mitigating the failure. As a result, we should always consider what can be done to reduce the "mean time to restore" for each failure mode and this is the intent of the consequence reduction task. For every "run to failure" or "no scheduled maintenance" decision, there are a number of things we should consider to reduce the consequences of the failure:

1. Spare parts - If we are considering running this component to failure, it may be a good idea to have this part stocked on site, or with a vendor who can deliver the part in an acceptable amount of time.

2. Job Plans - A well written job plan that includes lock-out tag-out, tools needed, and a clear step-by-step plan to facilitate replacement, including who is responsible for getting parts while the failed part is removed. This plan will go a long way in reducing down time for your critical asset while the repair or replacement task is performed.

3. By Pass Permit - When acceptable, it may be possible to safely by-pass the component until repair/replacement can be scheduled.

The following diagram represents some of the individual steps that take place for each emergency, or demand failure, at your plant.

Is There Room For Reducing Consequences?

- Equipment Fails
- Operator Troubleshoots
- Operator Contacts Maintenance
- Maintenance Responds
- Maintenance Troubleshoots
- Lock Out Tag Out Try Out
- Locate Parts Needed
- Order Parts Needed
- Make Repair
- Return LOTOTO
- Restart

FMECA
Selecting Maintenance Tasks

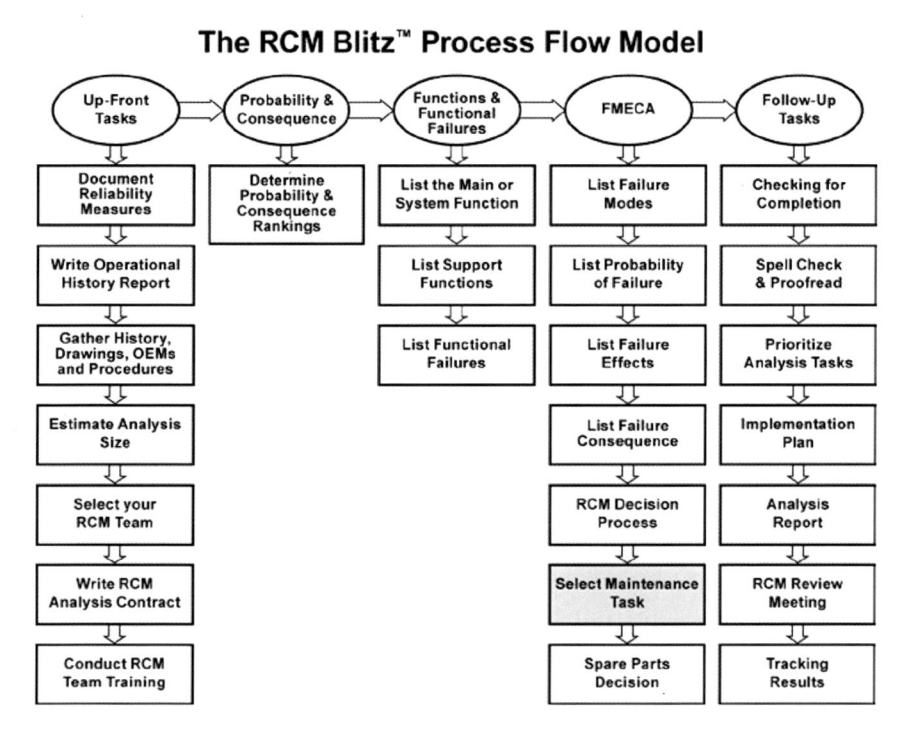

The RCM Blitz™ Process Flow Model

```
Up-Front Tasks → Probability & Consequence → Functions & Functional Failures → FMECA → Follow-Up Tasks
```

Up-Front Tasks	Probability & Consequence	Functions & Functional Failures	FMECA	Follow-Up Tasks
Document Reliability Measures	Determine Probability & Consequence Rankings	List the Main or System Function	List Failure Modes	Checking for Completion
Write Operational History Report		List Support Functions	List Probability of Failure	Spell Check & Proofread
Gather History, Drawings, OEMs and Procedures		List Functional Failures	List Failure Effects	Prioritize Analysis Tasks
Estimate Analysis Size			List Failure Consequence	Implementation Plan
Select your RCM Team			RCM Decision Process	Analysis Report
Write RCM Analysis Contract			**Select Maintenance Task**	RCM Review Meeting
Conduct RCM Team Training			Spare Parts Decision	Tracking Results

As we perform a RCM Blitz™ analysis, the main objective or outcome of the analysis is a complete maintenance strategy determined by reviewing all likely failure modes and using a structure decision process. This strategy identified by the RCM team, when implemented and performed by operations and maintenance, will ensure the inherent designed reliability of the asset.

One of the most amazing things about RCM is that once you truly master the art of facilitating the process, it becomes very simple and easy to manage. Plan for your events, follow the steps of the process in order, and soon you will have your first analysis completed and implemented.

I have worked in the field of maintenance and reliability my entire adult life. I have always enjoyed the challenge of designing, building, and maintaining equipment. I get the most enjoyment, however, from improving the process of how we do maintenance, and observing the results of improved reliability, specifically the change in culture that occurs when reliability changes people's lives. I have seen the implementation of a single RCM analysis change the culture of a business that had performed strictly reactive maintenance for thirty years into a group of true believers who could not wait to schedule their next RCM analysis. It is this energy that drives me to continue to learn, apply and instruct RCM.

As we make our way through the RCM process, our main goal is to develop a maintenance strategy to mitigate all probable failure modes for each component within the envelope of our analysis. In doing so, we consider the following types of maintenance and select the task that is best suited to ensure the highest level of reliability. Using the RCM Blitz™ methodology we consider the following types of maintenance:

1. On-Condition Maintenance (PdM)
2. Preventive Maintenance
3. Failure-Finding Tasks
4. Redesign
5. Run to Failure (Consequence Reduction Tasks)

On-Condition Maintenance
On-Condition maintenance is more widely called predictive maintenance, or PdM. In developing the RCM Blitz™ process and training materials, we made the decision to stick with the terminology used by Nowlan and Heap. Using their definition, on-condition maintenance is any maintenance task that looks to determine resistance to failure on a component for a specific failure mode. Based on the Potential Failure Curve (P-F Curve), on-condition tasks seek to detect a specific failure condition through the use of predictive maintenance techniques. These tasks can often be performed as the equipment is running, and if properly applied, we can detect failures as well as plan and schedule corrective maintenance, essentially eliminating unscheduled equipment failures and the resulting secondary damage associated with the failure.

When people think about on-condition maintenance, they usually think about the most commonly used predictive technologies (PdM) like vibration analysis, thermography, motor circuit analysis, and ultrasonic listening. What most people forget is that Stan Nowlan and Howard Heap included condition based inspection as on-condition tasks.

Condition Based Inspections are scheduled inspections put in place to detect the condition of a component or part using preset criteria to make fact based decisions. For example, checking the oil level in a gear box could be considered a condition based inspection if the gearbox has a sight glass that is clearly marked where the level of the oil should be.

Understanding the Complete P-F Curve

My first introduction to equipment reliability came in 1988, at Eastman Kodak Company, in Rochester, New York. Jerry Haggerty, one of the founding members of SMRP (Society of Maintenance and Reliability Professionals), had begun to assemble a steering committee of Kodak Maintenance professionals who would begin working together sharing information on equipment reliability.

I remember the emphasis Jerry put on understanding the P-F curve and the P-F interval. Jerry knew that if we could get our managers to understand the P-F curve, we could begin to make the transition into predictive technologies and reduce the amount of reactive maintenance being performed at our plants.

Nearly twenty years later, I can say with confidence that Jerry was somewhat correct. Understanding the P-F curve, the P-F interval, and the scheduling of predictive technologies is fundamental in building a sound PdM program.

The understanding of the P-F curve as most of us know it will help a maintenance or reliability manager to sell the need for predictive technologies such as vibration analysis, lubrication analysis, ultra-sound and IR inspections. This will also, if properly implemented, reduce the amount of reactive maintenance being performed. What the original P-F curve will not do is maximize the benefit of a PdM program.

Following the P-F curve most people are familiar with. The x-axis of the curve represents Time (T) or Operating Age, and the y-axis represents resistance to failure. Starting at the top left part of the curve and moving right we encounter point P, known as Potential Failure. This is the point in time that when using some form of Predictive Technologies one can first detect a defect has occurred and as a result the item is less resistant to failure.

Classic P-F Curve

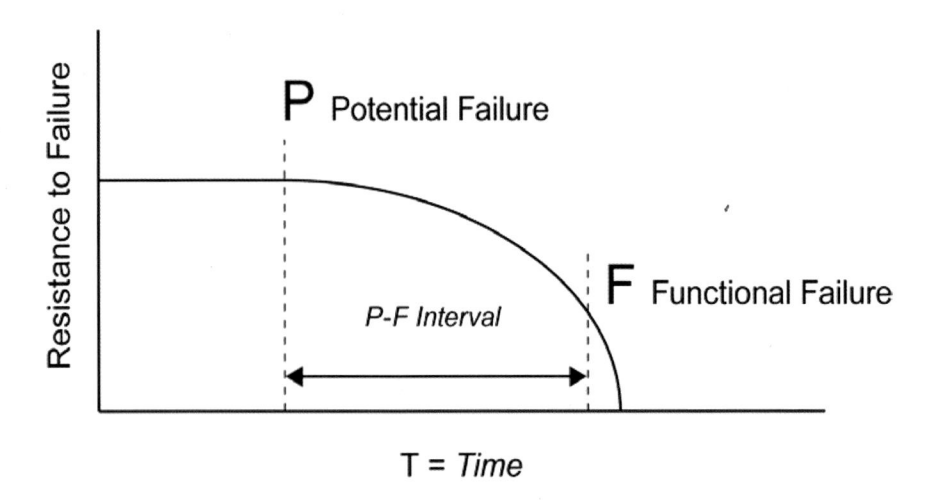

[Graph: Y-axis labeled "Resistance to Failure", X-axis labeled "T = Time". A curve starts flat and then drops. Point P marked "Potential Failure" at start of drop, point F marked "Functional Failure" further along. The horizontal distance between P and F is labeled "P-F Interval".]

As we continue to move right along this curve, resistance to failure continues to fall until we encounter point F, known as Functional Failure. This is the point in time when the components resistance to failure has deteriorated to a point where it can no longer perform its intended function.

The time elapsed between point P and point F is known as the P-F interval. The value of knowing the P-F interval of a component for a specific failure mode is that we now can set the interval of the condition based (PdM) inspection.

In setting the interval, we should now, with a high level of confidence, be able to detect the failure of this component, plan a replacement or restoration task and repair the component before the failure occurs. In doing so, we have replaced what was once a reactive task with a PdM task.

The introduction of the P-F Curve and on-condition PdM tasks provided a much needed innovative change in a world where Preventive Maintenance was viewed as the only option to avoid emergency/demand maintenance. Excitement around the P-F Curve quickly evolved into a new age of "proactive maintenance" for companies who could afford the new and costly predictive technologies associated with Predictive Maintenance. Companies who invested in technologies such as Vibration

Analysis, Lubrication Analysis, and Thermographic Analysis, paid large sums for the equipment and training to develop in-house Predictive Maintenance groups and not long after making these investments began sharing stories of success and the savings that could be generated from detecting failures, and the costly secondary damage associated with emergency maintenance.

Today, it would be no stretch at all to make the connection between the P-F Curve, Predictive Maintenance and the birth of SMRP, ReliabilityWeb.com, IMC, and Marts. As word on Predictive Maintenance spread around the world, PdM course offerings and PdM service providers exploded, making the new technologies both more attractive and affordable. By 1995, if you were benchmarking your company's maintenance organization, you could not be world class if you were not involved in predictive maintenance.

Something is Missing
Several years after working with Jerry Haggerty, I left Eastman Kodak to form Reliability Solutions, Inc., a consulting firm specializing in training people in reliability tools and measures. As part of our company services, we also offered on-site consulting and mentoring and it was at one of these on-site visits that I learned the P-F curve was incomplete.

Our client, in the past two years, had invested a substantial amount of money to develop a Predictive Maintenance Program and, while quite proud of that program, they also revealed that they were disappointed that it was not delivering the savings at a rate they had hoped for. Our client's PdM service provider collected data from hundreds of pieces of rotating equipment around their plant. They prepared reports for our client that showed nearly all of their rotating equipment was in the process of failure (someplace between points P and F). As trained, our client would then open a maintenance work order to schedule replacement of the asset prior to failure. Using precision alignment techniques, the rotating equipment would be replaced and to their extreme disappointment, months later they would be informed that the same asset was again failing. The P-F curve detailed next represents our client's experience with Predictive Technologies and the P-F Interval. Notice the saw tooth effect that designates each time the asset is replaced or repaired.

While the Saw Tooth P-F Curve still effectively eliminates running costly rotating equipment to failure, it can lull maintenance managers into the illusion that PdM is all maintenance has to offer regarding these types of failures. While one could celebrate that this company successfully detected and responded to three potential failures over a short period of time and avoided the costly secondary damage associated with each failure, I would want them to question why each failure occurred.

Saw Tooth P-F Curve
Resulting From Failure To Identify Specific Causes For Failure Modes

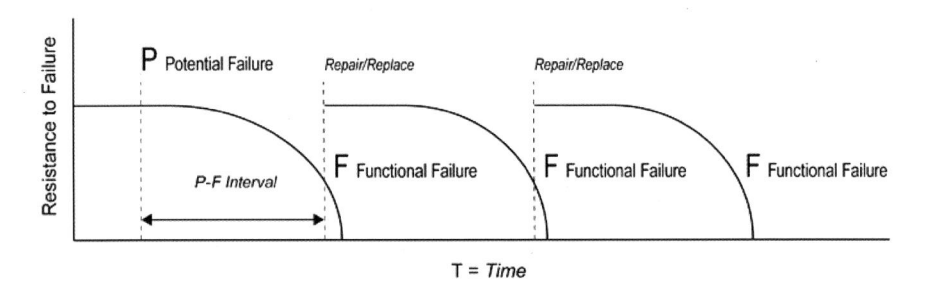

The most important thing we need to understand about the P-F Curve and the Saw Tooth P-F Curve is this:

- Detecting potential failure is not enough to consider your PdM program a success. For each detected potential failure we must also determine the specific cause of failure. We need to know, "What has caused this potential failure, and most important, Can this cause be eliminated?"

If you ask and answer the above questions, your maintenance organization, PdM service providers, and company, are ready to gain the full benefit of the Modified P-F Curve utilizing not only Predictive Maintenance but Pro-Active maintenance techniques and Reliability Tools.

Failure Modes that result in the Saw Tooth P-F Curve:

- Misalignment
- Soft Foot
- Pipe Stress
- Lack of Lubrication
- Improper Lubrication

- Lubrication Breakdown
- Undersized Foundations
- Improper Belt Tension - Too Tight/Too Loose
- Over Torque of Electrical Connections
- Dirt/Dust/Moisture Contamination of Electrical Connections
- Improper Sized Wiring, Overloads or Heaters
- Improper Torque of Piping Connections that Result in Leaks
- Improper Gasket Materials
- Improper Design or Application
- Poor Start Up or Shut Down
- Inadequate Cleaning
- Inadequate Operation or Not Operating to Standards

While each of these failure modes could be detected using some form of Predictive Technologies, and then corrected prior to total failure, if the failure mode is not properly identified the failure will occur again.

The above should clearly highlight the need to take your Predictive Maintenance program a step further by asking the above listed questions each time a component has been determined to have reached point P. In doing so, you can now pinpoint the specific cause of each failure and use RCM decision logic and sound Proactive Maintenance techniques to eliminate these causes and the saw tooth effect.

As we performed an RCM Blitz™ analysis of several assets at our clients facilities it became clear why some were not having the success they had expected from their PdM program. In working with their PdM service provider to set up their PdM program they had simply generated a list of assets for each specific technology, the list generated for critical assets, set up PdM routs and intervals for each asset based on the providers recommendations. In most cases, Vibration Analysis and Airborne Ultrasonic tasks were performed on a monthly basis, Theromgraphic inspections were set up on a quarterly basis, and Motor Current Evaluation was performed every six months. Not one single PdM inspection detailed the failure modes the tasks were looking to detect. While we all understood the P-F curve and the P-F interval we failed to understand or determine why the assets were failing over and over again.

While the technologies our client had invested in were successfully detecting failures, our client had never asked the service provider why the assets continued to fail over and over again. This is where the addition to the P-F curve comes in. In the representation below note the difference in this P-F curve. Starting at the far left at point D (Design), followed by point I (Installation) and moving right we have a very long flat line going between point I and point P (Potential Failure) - this is what we call the I-P interval. [2]

The I-P interval represents the time it takes move from the point of installation to the point where Potential Failure is first detected. The objective of all world-class maintenance and reliability organizations should be to work to maximize the I-P Interval. This can only be achieved through a thorough understanding of your assets, proactive maintenance techniques and reliability tools. In viewing the P-F curve in this manner it became clear to our client that a large percentage of the failure modes they were detecting through the use of predictive technologies could in fact be identified and eliminated using RCM and proactive maintenance techniques.

As an example, one of the failures our client was seeing over and over again was on a blower that was mounted to an undersized foundation. Each time they replaced the blower they used precision alignment to ensure the blower and motor sheaves were properly aligned. Without proper foundational support, continued stopping and starting of the blower over time resulted in misalignment and degradation of the blower and motor bearings. In performing the RCM Blitz analysis of this asset we listed all of the probable failure modes for the blower and determined that the blower base and foundation would need redesign to eliminate the failure mode. The result – a blower that had failed three times in eighteen months has not failed in over four years.

---

[2] I added Pont D to the Complete P-F curve following comments from Ron Moore on the original RCM Blitz™ book. Thanks Ron!

Asset Reliability Curve

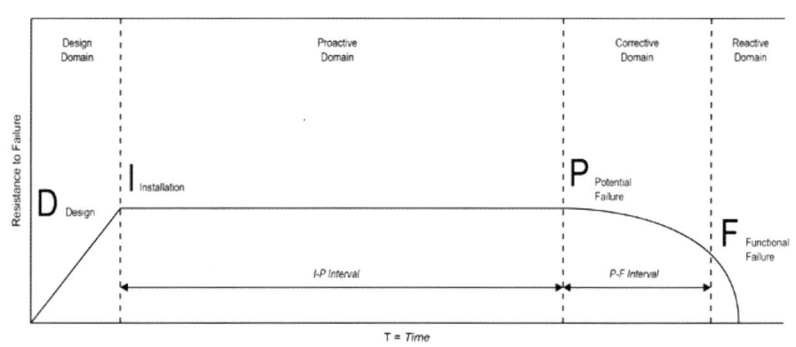

[Chart showing Resistance to Failure vs. Time, with domains labeled Design, Proactive, Corrective, and Reactive. Key points: D (Design), I (Installation), P (Potential Failure), F (Functional Failure). Intervals shown: I-P Interval and P-F Interval.]

The Value in Understanding the Modified P-F Curve

While many companies and maintenance organizations around the world have seen the value in understanding the original P-F curve, I want you all to understand the additional value provided by our Modified P-F Curve. To do this we start at the far right end of the P-F Curve at the point of complete failure (where the P-F curve contacts the x-axis).

Moving from here back to the left and up to point F (Functional Failure), this interval between Functional Failure and Failure is the interval where reactive maintenance takes place and is also known as the reactive domain. It's the area of time where this piece of rotating equipment starts smoking, shaking, stinking, and squealing. As a result we quickly send someone out to shut the asset down so that it can be replaced. Performing maintenance in this area is costly and minimizes maintenance effectiveness to less than ten percent.

Moving back to the left and up from point F we encounter point P. This is the well known P-F interval or the corrective domain, the time frame where Predictive Maintenance (PdM) can be employed to monitor fault progression. The value of performing maintenance here is we can detect when failures are in the process of occurring, then plan and schedule repair or replacement to minimize equipment damage and reduce operations down time. Performing maintenance in P-F interval provides a cost benefit that increases maintenance effectiveness to as high as fifty percent. This is accomplished by reducing secondary equipment damages that occurs when equipment is run to failure.

Tools and Techniques that can be employed in the corrective domain:

1. RCA – Root Cause Analysis
2. Planning and Scheduling
3. PdM Tools – To monitor fault progression if there are real time constraints
4. Consequence Reduction Techniques

Why focus efforts here?
The detection of potential failures (Point P) allows time to plan, schedule and execute corrective maintenance in a way that significantly reduces the costs incurred when we run our assets to failure. Root Cause Analysis can help us to identify and eliminate causes and improve the I-P interval of the asset.

We now move left on the P-F curve from point P (Potential Failure) back to point I (Installation). The I-P interval is the time frame from installation (I) to potential failure (P). This interval should take years to elapse provided the correct Proactive reliability tools are employed and precision maintenance techniques and tools are used at installation. Performing these Proactive Maintenance techniques will provide a cost benefit that increases maintenance effectiveness to one-hundred percent!

To reach this level of effectiveness one will need to understand how Proactive Maintenance Techniques and Reliability Tools can increase the I-P interval of your assets.

Understanding Proactive Maintenance Techniques and Reliability Tools

While it would take a full text book to be able to completely explain the value of each technique and tool, I will list each out here and provide a summary of how each can extend your I-P Interval.

> **Reliability Centered Maintenance RCM Blitz™** – RCM is a Reliability Tool that uses a structured team approach to analyze a process or piece of equipment. In performing a RCM analysis, your team will assess all likely failure modes for the asset and develop a maintenance strategy to mitigate the consequences for each failure mode. The value in performing RCM is the proactive assessment of these failure modes and the resulting tasks developed to eliminate reoccurring failures.

FMEA – Failure Modes and Effects Analysis – Similar to RCM, FMEA is a Reliability Tool used in the design phase to identify likely failure modes. In performing FMEA your design team will discuss these failure modes and attempt to design out failure modes that result from poor design and installation decisions.

Precision Alignment and Balancing – Precision maintenance tools are known for increasing the life of rotating equipment. While these tools have been available for several years, few of us have taken advantage of their use. Precision alignment and balancing will both dramatically reduce vibration that results in reoccurring failures of bearings, seals and couplings.

Installation Standards – Used for both new installation and maintenance, these standards are put in place to ensure proper craft skills are used when working on equipment/assets. Some examples of installation standards would be the identification of the proper type and grade of flange hardware and gasket material. Developing installation standards eliminates reoccurring failures, such as leaks, caused by using incorrect gasket material.

Torque Specifications – While almost everyone working in maintenance knows what a torque wrench is and what torque specifications are, they are seldom used. Leaking connections, loose rotating equipment, and sight glass failure are often the result of improper torque. While using a torque wrench and following the specifications may take more time, the resulting reliability will increase your I-P Interval.

Precision Tools – If you want to ensure proper maintenance and installation practices your people will need precision tools to do the work. As I work with companies I can quickly assess the level of understanding concerning reliability with a quick look in the tool boxes of their maintenance people. Hammers, channel-locks, pry bars and screw drivers alone will begin to ensure reliability. Precision work requires precision tools and if your people don't have these tools, don't expect your results to improve.

Finally moving all the far left we have point D. In the design phase of this complete P-F curve or Reliability Curve we have a number of tools available in the design phase to help us to design reliability into a process or piece of equipment. While companies around the world struggle to improve the reliability of their critical assets, it is important to understand that the reliability of your equipment starts with the design, is only ensured through a sound installation, and followed up by solid operating and maintenance techniques.

The following tools should be used at the time of design to build reliability into your system.

> **Reliability Centered Maintenance RCM Blitz™** – RCM is a Reliability Tool that works extremely well in the design phase of any project. Just like performing a RCM analysis on an existing asset it is imperative that a cross functional team with expert level experience be used to perform the analysis.
>
> **The Five Rights of Reliability** – Design it right, purchase it right, build it right, operate it right and maintain it right. An overall reliability program focused on educating employees at all levels and organizations on the importance of reliability. The five rights of reliability develops a reliability plan across engineering, purchasing, construction, operations and maintenance that clearly describes how each business unit can improve reliability.
>
> **Select Supplier Agreements** – Often a part of your reliability plan, select supplier agreements should be made consulting engineering, operations, maintenance and purchasing. These agreements should be developed using your company's reliability data while working with suppliers to provide the most robust and reliable assets. Inferior parts or components are a common cause for reoccurring failures.
>
> **Requirements Documents** – If this is not part of your companies capital design and engineering program it needs to be. Requirements documents are binding agreements written to ensure the highest level of reliability in design and installation. As an example many companies now have requirements documents written for the acceptable level of vibration on start up of new rotating equipment. The document will clearly state what that acceptable measure will be and the resulting action

taken if the requirement is not achieved. Again, the intent of these documents is to eliminate failure modes inherent to poor design or installation practices.

Design standards – Company design standards should always be used as a tool to improve equipment reliability. Used in combination with select suppliers, and requirements documents, design standards will help your company ensure all new installations are safe and reliable. Some examples of design standards that will eliminate reoccurring failure modes: standard mass requirements for pump foundations, standards requirements for piping supports, standards for starter panel installations.

Some Things to Work On

For those of us who have been directly involved in making the cultural changes in moving from reactive maintenance to predictive maintenance, we understand these changes take training and time. These changes do not take place overnight; they come in the form of small victories as people learn these techniques do work. As we now look to move back on the P-F curve to include and employ proactive maintenance techniques, a first step in the transition should be to require your PdM Technologists to list the Failure Mode associated with failures resulting equipment entering the P-F curve. In doing so we can identify and eliminate the failures that result in failure reoccurrence or the saw tooth P-F curve.

The most effective way to enter into and employ Proactive Maintenance techniques is to become involved in RCM. Reliability Centered Maintenance is the most effective way to develop a complete maintenance strategy that includes both Proactive and Predictive maintenance tasks, and it should be applied to all critical process equipment. RCM is the only way to quickly identify and eliminate reoccurring failures through redesign and effective preventive maintenance tasks. Correctly applied and implemented RCM will always provide an effective return on the money invested for training, analyses, and implementation.

Some simple things to think about along these same lines is the number of Failure Modes that can be detected using Predictive Technologies that could simply have been eliminated altogether had we taken the time to identify these failure modes using Reliability Centered Maintenance. While it is extremely important for all maintenance organizations to celebrate the detection of potential failures through Predictive Technologies it is far more important for us to eliminate failures whenever possible. Failure identification and elimination offers the greatest savings and presents your maintenance group as truly a world-class maintenance and reliability organization.

Preventive Maintenance
Preventive Maintenance (PM) is one of the most commonly used maintenance techniques and at the same time it is by far the most abused maintenance technique. In the United States, PM was developed and popularized to improve the reliability of military equipment in World War II. Following the war, PM was introduced to manufacturing equipment as a way to keep equipment running thus improving its reliability. While PM can be a very effective maintenance technique it must be applied to wear based components at the correct interval to be considered applicable and effective. Preventive Maintenance tasks should only be applied to components that fit conditional probability of failure patterns A-C noting this PM is only effective on approximately 11% of components at any given facility. I would also note at this point that of this 11% there are many cases where PdM tasks would be better suited for detecting many failure modes and allow for optimal life out of these components.

Types of PM Tasks
Preventive Maintenance tasks can be separated into two types or categories: Scheduled Rework and Scheduled Discard.

1. A **Scheduled Rework** task is a time based rebuild of a wear-based component. This component contains moving or stationary parts that wear over time and as a result if we understand the wear rate we can set up a preventive maintenance task to "rework or rebuild" the component.

2. A **Scheduled Discard** tasks are time based tasks put in place to discard or throw away parts or components and replace them with new. As an example one could set up a scheduled discard task to remove and discard v-belts replacing them with new using known wear rates for properly aligned and tensioned belts.

Failure Patterns: 1960s & 1970s Data

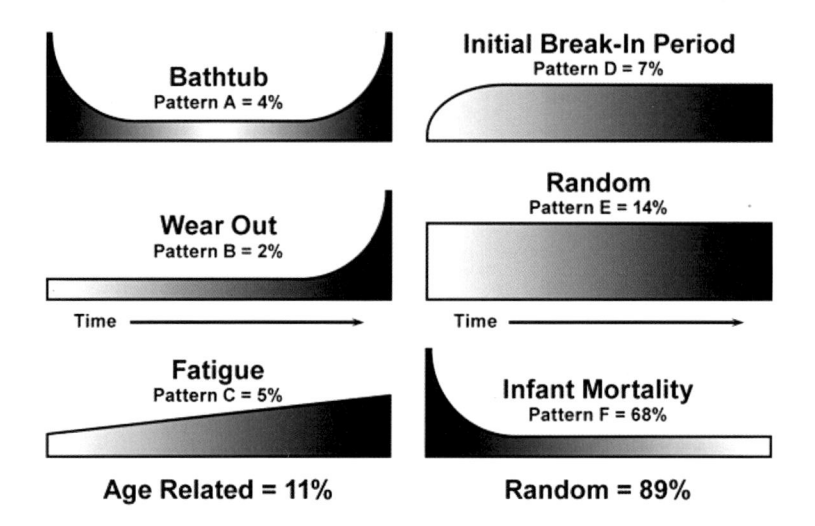

Bathtub
Pattern A = 4%

Initial Break-In Period
Pattern D = 7%

Wear Out
Pattern B = 2%

Random
Pattern E = 14%

Time →

Time →

Fatigue
Pattern C = 5%

Infant Mortality
Pattern F = 68%

Age Related = 11%

Random = 89%

Wear Based Failures
Conditional Probability of Fail A-C

Failure Pattern A

Failure Pattern A is known as the Bath Tub Curve and represents components that will suffer a period of early life failures, followed by an extended period of low probability random failures and then a rapid increase in conditional probability of failure caused by wear out. Electro-Mechanical components are good examples of this, items like limit switches and push buttons. If these items are properly installed, the electrical function of these components result in the early life portion of the failure pattern, components that survive the early life failures will then continue to operate for an extended period of time with a low level of random failures followed by the wear out section. This is where the spring, wheel, or arm of the limit switch becomes loose, fails to contact the striker or breaks and falls off. Nowlan and Heap reported that 4% of aircraft components fit failure pattern A. In a study I performed in 2003, using 80 RCM analyses, across 10 business sectors, with nearly 10,000 components, we reported 3% of the components fit failure pattern A.

Failure Pattern B

Failure Pattern B is known as the classic wear curve. I like to tell people that this is the failure pattern, as maintenance professionals, we wish every component fit. Failure pattern B components, if properly installed, should start and run for years with a low level of random failures until they reach a point where, as a result of wear based failure modes, the conditional probability of failure quickly increases. If one were to track the life of properly installed classic Failure Pattern B components, you would see a tight normal distribution of failures. From this distribution, we should be able to calculate the useful life of these components, a point where the component can be rebuilt or replaced based on known failure rate, and the pending consequences of running the item to failure.

Life as a maintenance professional would be easy if all the components in our plants followed Failure Pattern B. If this were the case, we could use precision maintenance techniques to properly install these components, we could then run several of the components to failure and determine the useful life of each. At this point, we would set a recommended interval to perform the PM, thus eliminating nearly every failure in the plant. The reality, however, is that Nowlan and Heap found only 2% of aircraft components fit failure pattern B. In my 2003 study, 3.5% of manufacturing components fit this distribution. Examples of failure pattern B components would be belts, sheaves, chains and sprockets.

Failure Pattern C

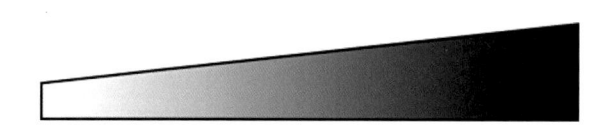

Failure Pattern C is known as the steady wear pattern. From the point when these components are installed, and put into service, the conditional probability of failure increases over time. Pipes, tires and clutches are good examples of failure pattern C components. Using the tires on your car as an example, as soon as you install new tires, the probability the tire will fail increases steadily. This would include road hazard failures, punctures, and over time road wear. Nowlan and Heap found that 5% of aircraft components fit failure pattern C. In the 2003 study, we found 6.5%.

Concerning the three wear-based failure patterns, we have a low of 11%, and a high of 13%, of component failures to which PM would be an effective maintenance strategy at ensuring the designed reliability of the asset. Of this 11 to 13%, it is important to remember that precision maintenance techniques must be applied to ensure the PM tasks are both applicable and effective. Add to this advancements in PdM technologies, and the percentage of applicable PM's is even less. For example, using the corrosion, erosion or abrasion of piping as a failure pattern C component failure, it would be far more effective to use Uniform Thickness Testing, a Non Destructive task, to address these failures.

Random Based Failure Patterns D-F
With only 11 to 13 percent of equipment failures being wear based that leaves a rather large 87 to 89 percent as Random Based. This is where a thorough understanding of the P-F curve, Predictive Technologies and Precision Maintenance becomes important as these are the tools you will need to use to mitigate random based failures. While the wear based failure patterns typically represent simple, single cell components such as belts, sheaves, brake pads, and turbine engine compressor blades, the Random Based pattern are often more complex components like hydraulic, pneumatic and electrical devices. Age is not a factor for these failure curves so time based maintenance for items that fit these distributions would only be applicable for hidden or EHS related items, where failure could result in catastrophic consequences.

Failure Pattern D

Known as the "Best New" failure pattern, this pattern shows little to no conditional probability of failure when the component is first installed and put into service. The conditional probability of failure then quickly rises to a low level of random failures. Both the United Airline study, as well as my own, found that 7% of the items fit failure pattern D. It is thought that hydraulic and pneumatic components fit failure pattern D. Items that fit this failure pattern can be maintained using PdM, provided they have a useful P-F interval where potential failures can be detected and replacement can be both planned and scheduled.

Failure Pattern E

This failure pattern is totally random, having a constant probability of failure at all ages. Items that fit this failure pattern can be maintained using PdM provided they have a useful P-F interval where potential failures can be detected and replacement can be both planned and scheduled. My 2003 study showed that 13% of components fit failure pattern E. The Nowlan and Heap study found 14%. The most common examples of Pattern E failure modes result from human error. How does one predict that someone is about to start a pump without first opening a suction valve? Another example would be the ball bearing, while most would be tempted to state that bearings wear out, the ball bearing is nearly perfect in design, the balls are surrounded by lubricant and if properly designed, installed, operated and maintained there should be no wear at all provided the lubricant remains in good condition. But add humans into the equation and we now have a very random set of failures.

Failure Pattern F

Known as the infant mortality pattern, these items have a high probability of failure at installation and provided they survive start-up or burn-in, the conditional probability of failure quickly drops to a low level of random failure. Electrical components fit failure pattern F. Many of these failures, depending on service, can be detected using PdM technologies such as Thermographic Imaging and Motor Circuit Analysis. The infant mortality portion of this distribution can also be reduced by having well trained/certified skilled trades combined with sound job plans for replacement/installation. Failure Pattern F represents

67% of components in the 2003 study and 68% of the Nowlan and Heap study.

Setting Task Intervals for On-Condition Tasks[3]

Setting the intervals for an on-condition task can be accomplished using a couple of different methods. The first method, and the one I always employ when facilitating RCM analyses, is to use some industry based standards for each technology. For example, if we were working to develop a task for the failure mode of a bearing that turned 1800 rpm, we would encourage the team to set up an on-condition task to perform vibration analysis on a monthly basis.

Below we have listed several common PdM technologies and the industry standards interval for each.

PdM Technology	Standard Interval
Vibration Analysis	Monthly
Thermography	Quarterly
Oil Analysis	Quarterly
Airborne Ultrasound	Quarterly
Structure-borne Ultrasound	Quarterly
Motor Circuit Analysis (Online)	Quarterly
Motor Circuit Analysis (Offline)	Semi-Annually

Another method involves the use of Weibull statistics and the Monte Carlo simulation. Once the FMECA library is populated with the Failure Modes and Tasks Selections, the interval can be calculated by adding some additional levels of detail. Software like Availability Workbench™ can be used to create a comprehensive model of the equipment maintenance plan. Once the model is populated, it can be analyzed to see if the goals and objectives can be accomplished with this particular strategy.

First, the effect(s) of the failure need to be monetized. Cost per event and costs per hour during the event have to be populated into the model. Then the cost of the inspection and probability of detection have to be factored into the model. Finally an estimation of the failure profile for that particular failure mode has to be entered. This is accomplished by

---

[3] Andy Page, CMRP, is vice-president at Allied Reliability. Andy is an expert in condition based maintenance and has developed courses in PdM techniques for Allied. Andy assisted in writing this section.

entering the β (beta) value (a.k.a. - shape profile) and the η (eta) value (a.k.a. - Characteristic Life) of the failure mode. Once all of this information is entered, the Monte Carlo simulation can be run and the optimal inspection interval can be calculated based on the acceptable risk levels previously defined in the model.

While the industry standard intervals are significantly older than the calculated intervals, they are still a very close match for typical failures. This is an excellent indicator that the industry standard intervals are pretty close to what the calculated intervals would be for typical failures in typical situations. Of course, where the failure effects are not typical, or cost of downtime doesn't qualify as "typical", then an optimized calculation is necessary to simultaneously mitigate risk and cost.

Typical Failure Mode Example:
Component: A/C Induction Motor with Rolling Element Bearings (grease lubricated)
Failure Mode: Bearing - Fatigued - Age/Cycles
Cost of Downtime: $5,500 per hour (typical industrial average)
β Value: 1.1 (indicating a fatigue failure)
η Value: 61,320 hours (indicating a typical bearing life of 7 years)

Industry Standard Interval: 720 hours (30 days)
Calculated Inspection Interval: 703 hours (29 days)

Failure Finding Tasks
Failure Finding tasks are time based maintenance tasks put into place to find failures of hidden function components that have already occurred but are not evident to the operating crew as they perform their normal duties.

As we look at our facilities, there are two categories of hidden function components:

1. Passive Components - These devices are typically installed to protect the system and activate when a specific condition exists. A pressure relief valve set to relieve at 300 psi should activate when an over pressure condition of 300 psi exists and if the normal operating condition of this system is 180 psi, we have no idea if the intended function is still in working order. As a result, we have a regulated failure finding task to have the valve tested by a certified shop to ensure the valve opens/relieves at 300 psi.

2. Stand-By/Redundant Components - These devices are in stand-by condition waiting to take over should the primary device fail. During normal operating condition we have no idea if the stand-by component will work. This failure will not be evident to the operating crew as they perform their normal duties. To manage this failure mode, we should set up a failure-finding task to test the stand-by to ensure it functions properly.

While it is extremely important to identify every hidden function component within your facility, it is even more important to understand the potential consequences should the hidden failure go unnoticed. Hidden function devices are most often installed to protect your site, equipment, and employees from the catastrophic consequences that result when protective hidden devices fail to activate.

Examples of Hidden Function Components:

1. Relief Valves
2. Emergency Stop Switches
3. Fire Alarms
4. Safety Showers
5. Eye Baths
6. Rupture Discs
7. Pressure Switches
8. Level Switches
9. Level Probes
10. Fire Extinguishers
11. Smoke Detectors
12. Sprinkler Systems
13. PLC Battery Back Up
14. Toxic Gas Detectors
15. Explosive Gas Detectors
16. Exit Signs
17. Emergency Lighting
18. Redundant/Back-up Components
19. Flame Arrestors
20. Conservation Vents
21. Secondary Containment
22. CO2 Detectors
23. Fire Escapes
24. Emergency Brakes
25. Spare Tire
26. Hazard Lights
27. Overloads
28. Fuses
29. Fusible Links
30. Fire Doors

Determining the Interval/Frequency of Failure-Finding Tasks
Whenever we have a component that is subject to functional failure that is not evident to the operating crew as they perform their normal duties, a scheduled task is necessary to protect the availability of that function. While these failures may have no immediate consequences, the undetected failure increases the exposure to possible multiple failure. As a result, if no other type of task is applicable or effective at mitigating the failure, we must put into place a failure-finding task intended to detect functional failure that has already occurred but is not evident.

The objective of these tasks is to ensure adequate availability of the hidden function and this availability depends on the nature of the function and the consequences of possible multiple failures. This being said, the three most common ways to determine failure-finding task intervals are as follows:

1. Follow government or agency required intervals (component/service specific).

2. Follow Industry Standards for each component type and service.

3. Perform Failure Finding Task calculations based on anticipated failure rates, proposed inspection intervals, and expected survival rate at the proposed interval.

FMECA
Spare Parts

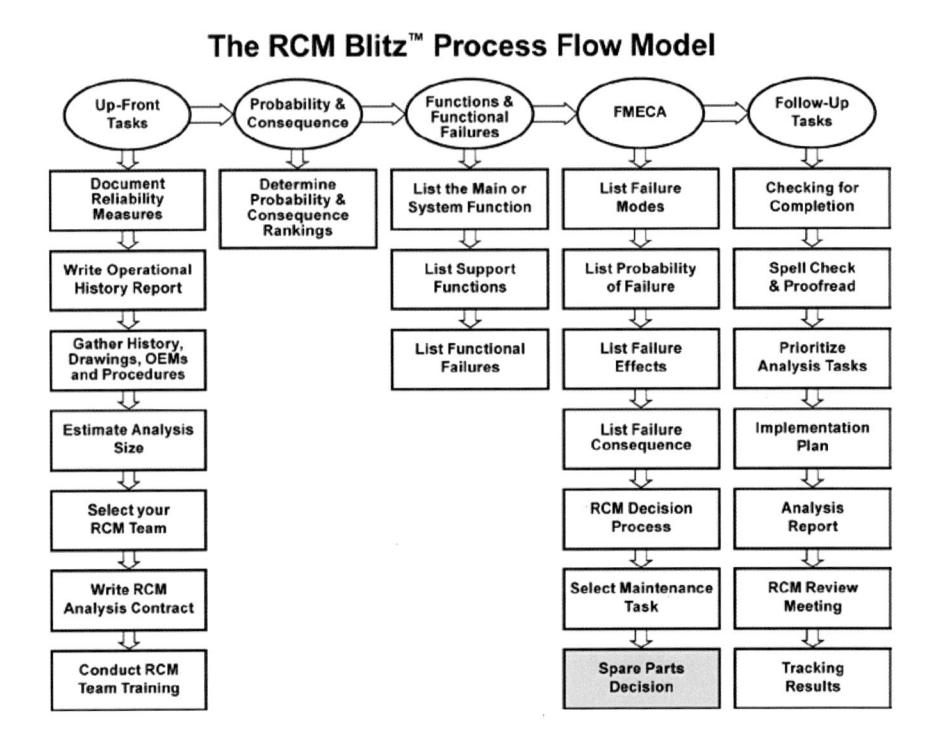

The RCM Blitz™ Process Flow Model

Up-Front Tasks	Probability & Consequence	Functions & Functional Failures	FMECA	Follow-Up Tasks
Document Reliability Measures	Determine Probability & Consequence Rankings	List the Main or System Function	List Failure Modes	Checking for Completion
Write Operational History Report		List Support Functions	List Probability of Failure	Spell Check & Proofread
Gather History, Drawings, OEMs and Procedures		List Functional Failures	List Failure Effects	Prioritize Analysis Tasks
Estimate Analysis Size			List Failure Consequence	Implementation Plan
Select your RCM Team			RCM Decision Process	Analysis Report
Write RCM Analysis Contract			Select Maintenance Task	RCM Review Meeting
Conduct RCM Team Training			Spare Parts Decision	Tracking Results

Very few RCM methodologies have ever considered equipment spares as part of the RCM process. I firmly believe that no maintenance strategy is complete without recommendations regarding spare parts.

When I was first performing RCM analyses for Eastman Kodak in Rochester, NY, we had performed a RCM analysis on a piece of critical equipment and were in the process of implementing the tasks identified in the RCM analysis when an I/O board for the machine PLC failed and as a result the machine shut down. When the machine shut down, operations contacted maintenance to troubleshoot, locate the failure and repair the equipment. Once maintenance had determined the I/O board had failed, they contacted the stockroom in hopes of locating the spare board, installing it and restarting the process. What they found out was that this part was no longer in stock. Apparently the part had been in stock at one time but the board had not been used in three years so it was deleted from stock. We now had to depend on purchasing to locate the vendor of this board and have one shipped as soon as possible. Our equipment would be down until this board was located, shipped and installed. Over the next two hours, we waited to hear on the progress of this part and the next contact from purchasing was not good. Seems the board we were trying to locate was "no longer available from company A". The part was obsolete!

Mean Time To Restore has now gone from 2 hours to who knows when! The price on the original board was three hundred dollars while the price of the equipment being down was 10 times that per hour. Worse than this, in performing the RCM analysis, our team had considered the failure of this component and made the correct decision of Run To Failure. As a maintenance or operations manager now waiting on locating an obsolete part, the run to failure decision seemed insane.

I have told this story many times and each time I share it, I hear four more stories just like it! Seems spare parts are a common problem when it comes to manufacturing facilities.

This being said, every argument has two sides, and if your responsibilities include purchasing and storeroom inventories you may have goals that are very different from those of a maintenance manager. The parts we keep in the storeroom all have a cost, it costs money to purchase the parts, it costs money for the store room and the people who work there, and each part or dollar in the inventory results in a tax burden on your company. The plain reality is maintenance spares should be kept to a necessary minimum and we can not possibly have a spare part for every asset at our plants.

Making Spare Parts Decisions
If you're looking to have a direct impact on the amount of parts and money tied up in your spare parts inventory, RCM will help, but the progress will be slow. The best way to quickly reduce your inventory is to begin by choosing select suppliers for all critical components. For example, if you work for a chemical company, chances are you may have as many as 8 different brands of centrifugal pumps, 6 different brands of motors, 5 different brands of ball valves and 12 brands of actuators. If you quickly want to reduce your inventory, choose 1 or 2 select suppliers for each. If you only allow 2 brands of centrifugal pumps, you now only have to carry the spares for these two brands. Starting with select suppliers will at first be a challenge, but in the end everyone, including purchasing, operations, and maintenance will be happy.

While we review spares as part of the RCM Blitz™ process, it should be understood we are reviewing the spares for a single critical asset so we never take into consideration the actual number of specific components your company has in service at any given time.

So, as we consider spare parts decisions we look at the following criteria:

1. Does this part have a known age or useful life?
2. Can the failure of this part be detected through the use of PdM?
3. Does the part cost more than the downtime resulting from its failure?
4. What is the probability of this part failing?
5. What is the consequence of this failure on your business?
6. Is this part still available through a vendor or is it obsolete?

In taking the above items into consideration, make one of the following spare parts recommendations:

1. Stock the part on site.
2. Stock the part at a vendor who can guarantee delivery in an acceptable amount of time.
3. Buy the part when needed.

CHAPTER 6
Follow-Up Tasks

Completing Your RCM Analysis

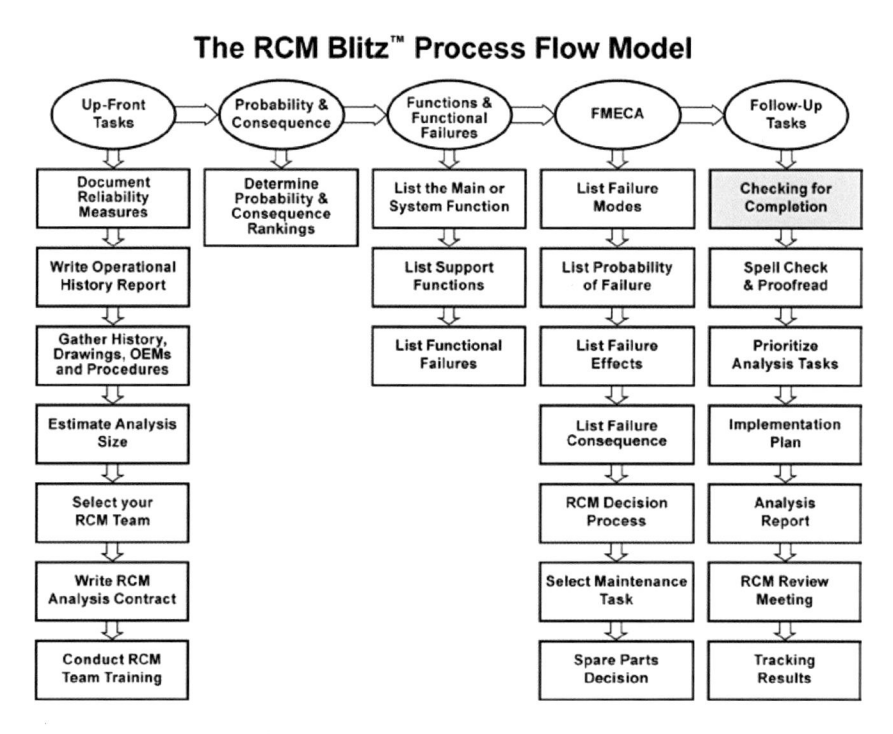

The RCM Blitz™ Process Flow Model

Up-Front Tasks	Probability & Consequence	Functions & Functional Failures	FMECA	Follow-Up Tasks
Document Reliability Measures	Determine Probability & Consequence Rankings	List the Main or System Function	List Failure Modes	Checking for Completion
Write Operational History Report		List Support Functions	List Probability of Failure	Spell Check & Proofread
Gather History, Drawings, OEMs and Procedures		List Functional Failures	List Failure Effects	Prioritize Analysis Tasks
Estimate Analysis Size			List Failure Consequence	Implementation Plan
Select your RCM Team			RCM Decision Process	Analysis Report
Write RCM Analysis Contract			Select Maintenance Task	RCM Review Meeting
Conduct RCM Team Training			Spare Parts Decision	Tracking Results

Completing a thorough RCM analysis comes only with a complete review of each of the support function components for each functional failure listed under the main function and a final review of each passive or hidden function component that may not have a direct impact on main functional failures.

As an example, many pump installations will have a low-flow shutdown switch to protect the pump from running dry or dead head, should this device fail in a state that would not detect the low-flow condition, it would in no way impact the main function of the pump.

Function 1 - Cooling Water Pump Main Function - To be able to pump cooling water at a rate of 120 gallons per/minute while meeting all quality, health, safety or environmental standards.

Function 2 - Low Flow Switch Support Function - To be capable of shutting down the pump in the event of a low flow condition for more than one minute

Cooling Water Pump Main Functional Failures
1.1 Unable to pump cooling water at all
1.2 Unable to pump cooling water at a rate of 120 gpm
1.3 Unable to maintain quality standards
1.4 Unable to maintain health, safety or environmental standards

In the event the low flow switch were failed in a state that it could not detect a low flow condition, the failure would not be evident during normal operating conditions. Its normal operating condition is running, pumping cooling water to various plant equipment. In this state, with the switch failed, the pump would continue to run. We could pump cooling water at the desired rate and the failure in no way impacts quality or HSE. Its failure in no way impacts any of the above listed main functional failures.

This failure now creates a number of questions that need to be asked:

1. What is the purpose or function of this device?
   Its function is to protect the pump from catastrophic failure.

2. What are the potential consequences of this failure?
   In the event the component failed, we could run the pump dry, or dead head the pump. This would result in a quick unexpected failure of the pump and the loss of cooling water to the plant.

3. Should there be a task in place to ensure the function of this device?

Looking at the potential consequences of the component failing in this state, its failure modes should be reviewed. To do this we will need to address the functional failure of the low-flow switch.

Low Flow Switch Functional Failure
2.1 Incapable of shutting down the pump in the event of a low flow condition

Failure Mode
2.1.1 Cooling water pump low flow switch failed in closed condition
Once we have completed a final review of all passive or hidden function components, the analysis portion of the RCM is complete. We will now move on to review the complete analysis for accuracy, spelling and then work to create the RCM implementation plan.

Follow Up Tasks
Spell Check and Proofread Your RCM Analysis

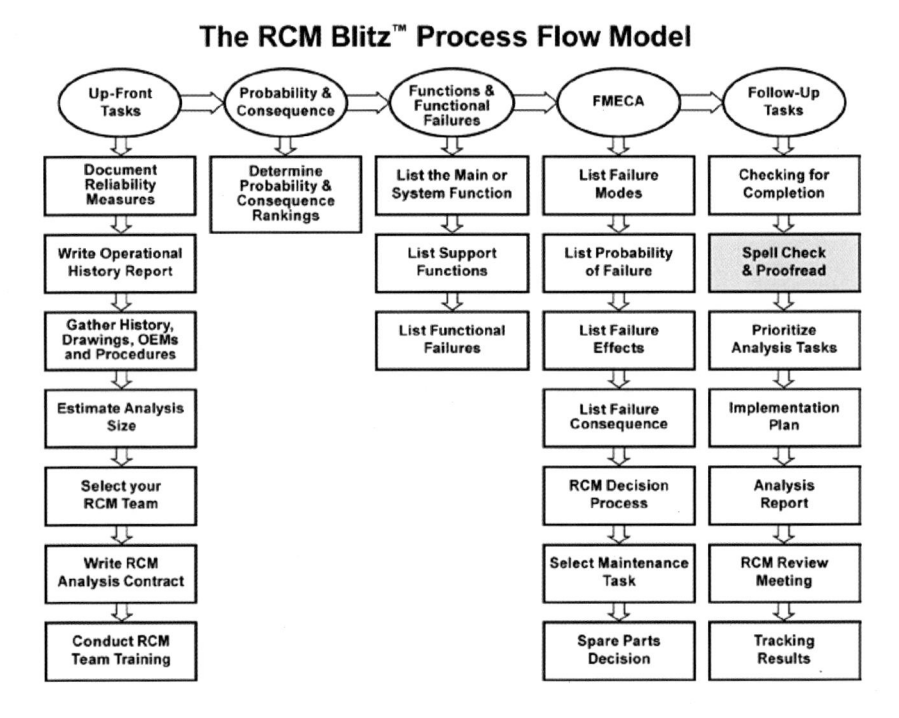

The RCM Blitz™ Process Flow Model

Up-Front Tasks	Probability & Consequence	Functions & Functional Failures	FMECA	Follow-Up Tasks
Document Reliability Measures	Determine Probability & Consequence Rankings	List the Main or System Function	List Failure Modes	Checking for Completion
Write Operational History Report		List Support Functions	List Probability of Failure	**Spell Check & Proofread**
Gather History, Drawings, OEMs and Procedures		List Functional Failures	List Failure Effects	Prioritize Analysis Tasks
Estimate Analysis Size			List Failure Consequence	Implementation Plan
Select your RCM Team			RCM Decision Process	Analysis Report
Write RCM Analysis Contract			Select Maintenance Task	RCM Review Meeting
Conduct RCM Team Training			Spare Parts Decision	Tracking Results

Your completed RCM analysis is a living document. No RCM analysis can include every failure that could ever occur, also other people, from time to time, will view your work. Knowing this, each completed RCM analysis should be both accurate and professional. The best way to ensure this is through a thorough proof reading and spell check of each analysis.

Try to be as accurate as possible in facilitating and entering the data into the RCM database. I have developed the habit of performing a spell check at each break in the RCM process. This keeps the final review process to a minimum.

First perform a computer driven spell check of the RCM document and print out the FMECA portion of the analysis for review. Invite one or two of your team members to review the document, then enter corrections into the database. Following spell checking in the database, print a hard copy for a more thorough final review.

Follow Up Tasks
Prioritization and RCM Implementation

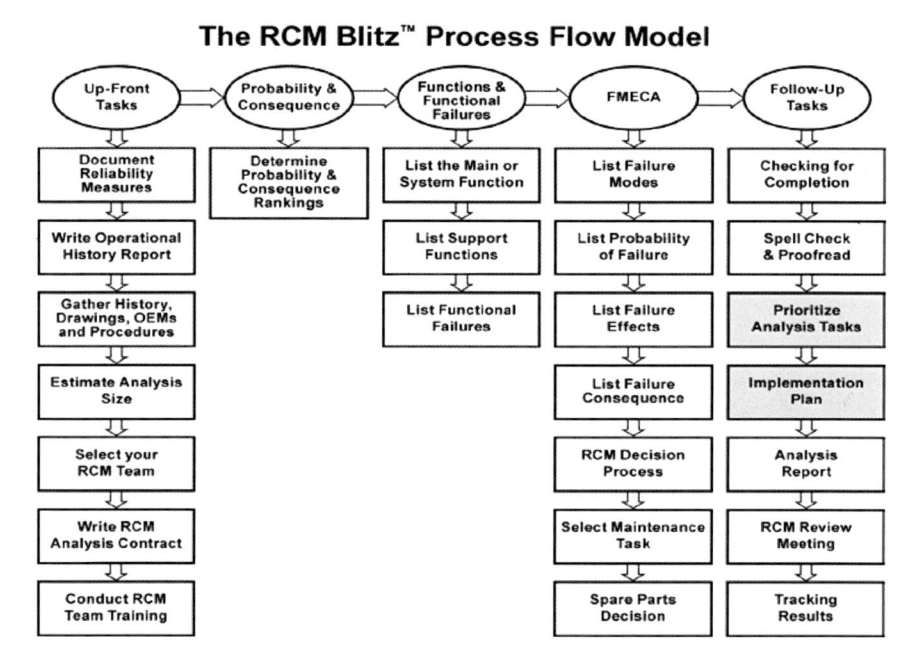

The RCM Blitz™ Process Flow Model

```
Up-Front Tasks → Probability & Consequence → Functions & Functional Failures → FMECA → Follow-Up Tasks
```

Up-Front Tasks	Probability & Consequence	Functions & Functional Failures	FMECA	Follow-Up Tasks
Document Reliability Measures	Determine Probability & Consequence Rankings	List the Main or System Function	List Failure Modes	Checking for Completion
Write Operational History Report		List Support Functions	List Probability of Failure	Spell Check & Proofread
Gather History, Drawings, OEMs and Procedures		List Functional Failures	List Failure Effects	Prioritize Analysis Tasks
Estimate Analysis Size			List Failure Consequence	Implementation Plan
Select your RCM Team			RCM Decision Process	Analysis Report
Write RCM Analysis Contract			Select Maintenance Task	RCM Review Meeting
Conduct RCM Team Training			Spare Parts Decision	Tracking Results

Prioritize Analysis Tasks

Using the information developed while determining the criticality of each failure mode, you can now prioritize each task. Failure Modes that have a High probability of occurring, and High consequence to your business should they occur, have a criticality ranking of 1 and the resulting task will be considered priority 1. A failure mode with a Low probability of occurrence and a Medium consequence to your business should it occur, will receive a criticality ranking of 4 and the resulting tasks will receive a priority 4 rank. Knowing the priority ranking of each task, we can now assign each priority a specific due date and assign the task for implementation.

RCM Implementation

Long before I threw my hat into the world of RCM facilitators, people had determined that implementation was the graveyard of most RCM efforts. I would like to be able to say that I have never been part of a failed Reliability Centered Maintenance effort but I would be a liar if I did. The reality is, I have spent more time trying to make implementation somehow easy and painless than I have trying to make the analysis process faster.

Implementation is the most important part of every world class RCM effort and if you want to understand just how important implementation is, consider the following two facts:

1. I have trained, mentored and facilitated for companies who no longer have a RCM effort in place. Each of these companies have one thing in common, they did not implement the tasks identified in the RCM analyses they performed.

2. I have trained, mentored, and facilitated for several companies who still have successful RCM efforts in place. Each of these companies either found a way to implement a task or called to have us assist in implementing the tasks they identified in their RCM analyses.

Over the past fifteen years, I have developed a few phrases that I share with companies as I provide RCM facilitations and training. When it comes to implementation, I like to say the following, "Performing a RCM analysis is very similar to exercise. It's something you do in preparation for a real event". The real event is implementation. You get something back when you implement, a return on your investment in improved reliability.

Perfecting Implementation
Now that I have scared the masses, I would like to say RCM implementation does not have to be difficult. In fact, I think it's simple really - Leadership - Structure - Discipline, sound familiar?

Leadership - When it comes to implementing your RCM tasks, you should first make one person responsible for tracking the implementation of your RCM tasks. This person will be your RCM implementation manager. He/she will work with the RCM team to develop the implementation plan. As part of this plan, each task will be assigned to a specific individual with an assigned due date.

Each week, the Implementation manager will update the RCM task spreadsheet and communicate implementation progress to the RCM team and business managers.

Structure - The structure portion is very easy as the RCM database provides the structure necessary to assign every task to specific individuals, each task having its own specific due date based on task priority.

Discipline - This involves setting due dates and completing tasks on or before the scheduled date. The trick in completing your implementation is to set up your plan and stick to it. RCM should only be performed on critical assets and improving the reliability of your critical assets should be a top priority.

Setting Up For Success

The average, weeklong RCM analysis develops around 150 individual tasks that need to be implemented. If you're using a good RCM database, the software will separate each individual task, allow you to prioritize each task, assign each task, set a due date for each task, and track completion of each task. You need to plan ahead when it comes to managing resources necessary to implement the RCM tasks.

As a general rule, if it took your RCM team one week to perform your RCM analysis, it will take three weeks to implement 80% of those tasks, understanding that part of the remaining twenty percent may require a small capital project that will take time for approval, planning and execution. I also urge companies to complete 80% of their first RCM before starting a second RCM. In the same way you plan to perform a RCM analysis by setting up a conference room, inviting people, and clearing schedules, at the same time you should be planning the resources necessary to implement the tasks that result from your analysis.

For each RCM analysis, you will need someone capable of writing sound electrical, mechanical and operational procedures and job plans. This person will not only need to be able to write the procedures but they should also be able to attach the procedure to a CMMS (Computerized Maintenance Management System) and set task frequencies. In most cases, these procedures can be completed by a maintenance planner or lead person and production supervisor. Once your PM, PdM, Operational Inspections and Job Plans have been completed, the bulk of your implementation is complete.

This being said, I offer the following six suggestions for seamless task implementation:

1. Identify Your Implementation Manager - **This person will track, drive and report the progress of your implementation plan.**

2. Clearly Describe Your Expectations for Implementing Tasks - **To what detail should tasks be written? If you don't make this clear at this point, you will find yourself rewriting PM tasks down the**

road. Show the people responsible for implementing tasks good examples of PM's, and where they can find more good examples.

3. Set Up Implementation Progress Meetings - **Regular implementation progress meetings should be set up on a monthly basis. At the meeting, the implementation manager will report to the team the progress that has been made implementing analysis tasks.**

4. Report Implementation Progress to Managers - **The implementation manager should report progress to business managers to keep them posted on the RCM process.**

5. Conduct a Final Review Meeting - **Business managers, the RCM Team, and the Implementation team should be invited. The completion of this analysis should be celebrated.**

6. Audit the Completion of Tasks - **Remember its one thing to implement tasks, it's another to actually do them. Random audits should be performed on implemented tasks to ensure they are actually being completed.**

Follow-Up Tasks
Creating the RCM Analysis Report

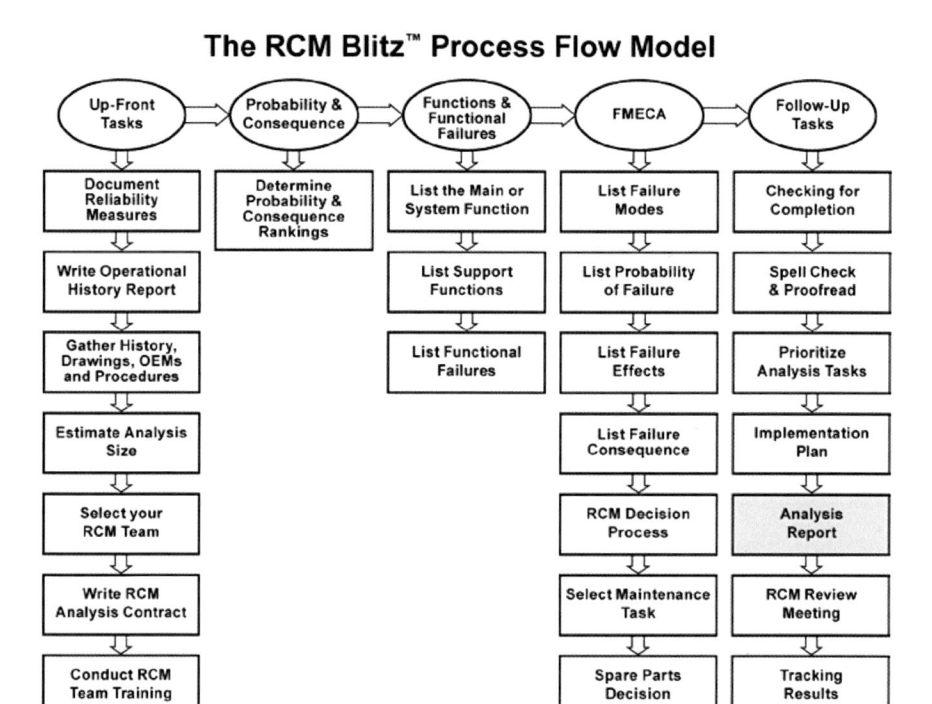

The RCM Blitz™ Process Flow Model

```
Up-Front Tasks → Probability & Consequence → Functions & Functional Failures → FMECA → Follow-Up Tasks
```

Up-Front Tasks:
- Document Reliability Measures
- Write Operational History Report
- Gather History, Drawings, OEMs and Procedures
- Estimate Analysis Size
- Select your RCM Team
- Write RCM Analysis Contract
- Conduct RCM Team Training

Probability & Consequence:
- Determine Probability & Consequence Rankings

Functions & Functional Failures:
- List the Main or System Function
- List Support Functions
- List Functional Failures

FMECA:
- List Failure Modes
- List Probability of Failure
- List Failure Effects
- List Failure Consequence
- RCM Decision Process
- Select Maintenance Task
- Spare Parts Decision

Follow-Up Tasks:
- Checking for Completion
- Spell Check & Proofread
- Prioritize Analysis Tasks
- Implementation Plan
- Analysis Report
- RCM Review Meeting
- Tracking Results

The RCM Analysis Report is easily created by printing out the documents created in the RCM Blitz™ Database. Print each report from the database and place them in three ring binders with tabs indicating each major report.

1. Operational History Report
2. Functions and Functional Failures
3. FMECA
4. Predictive and Preventive Tasks
5. Redesigns
6. Consequence Reduction Tasks
7. Spare Parts
8. Troubleshooting Guide
9. Implementation Plan

Follow-Up Tasks
RCM Review Meeting

The RCM Blitz™ Process Flow Model

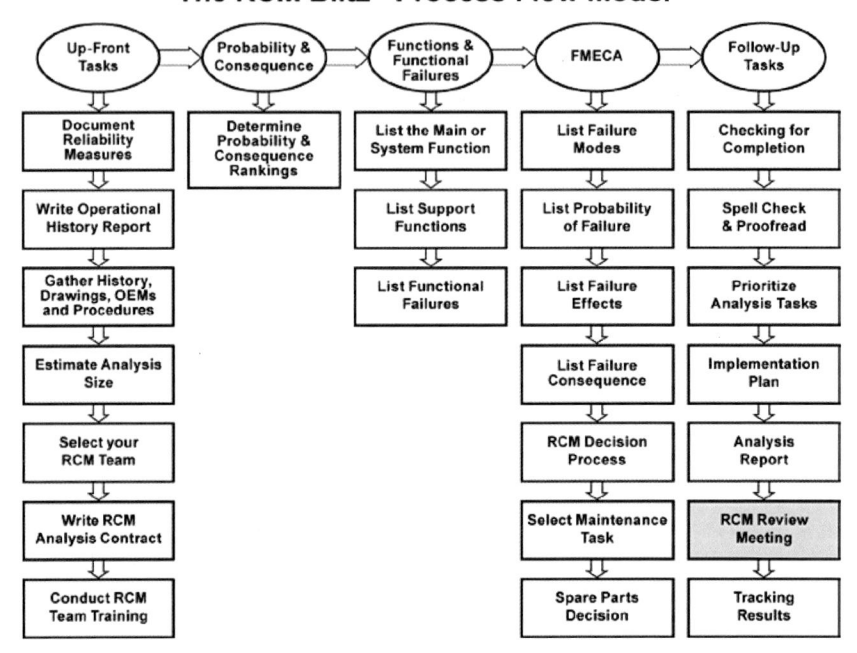

Up-Front Tasks	Probability & Consequence	Functions & Functional Failures	FMECA	Follow-Up Tasks
Document Reliability Measures	Determine Probability & Consequence Rankings	List the Main or System Function	List Failure Modes	Checking for Completion
Write Operational History Report		List Support Functions	List Probability of Failure	Spell Check & Proofread
Gather History, Drawings, OEMs and Procedures		List Functional Failures	List Failure Effects	Prioritize Analysis Tasks
Estimate Analysis Size			List Failure Consequence	Implementation Plan
Select your RCM Team			RCM Decision Process	Analysis Report
Write RCM Analysis Contract			Select Maintenance Task	**RCM Review Meeting**
Conduct RCM Team Training			Spare Parts Decision	Tracking Results

There is nothing more disappointing for me, as a RCM Practitioner, than facilitating a RCM analysis for a company and then watching the results of that RCM sit and rot like old fruit on the vine. One of the first analyses I facilitated as a consultant was on a critical process for a company who will remain nameless. In facilitating that analysis, the RCM team made some very simple recommendations that would have had a drastic impact on equipment reliability and product quality. The recommendations were what I would consider the lowest hanging fruit I have ever seen and as the RCM team presented our findings to company management you could feel the excitement from everyone in the room. This RCM was going to be a slam dunk and the resulting excitement generated a quick plan to train facilitators and begin performing more analyses. In six months time, this company had trained 28 RCM facilitators and completed over thirty RCM analyses. In that same time frame, not one single task from any of the thirty analyses had been implemented. There were millions of dollars in potential savings in these tasks but we failed to communicate the importance of implementation. In the following thirty days, this company suffered a downturn in business. They began looking for places to cut money and their RCM program was one of the first cuts. I use the failure of this effort as a learning experience for all of my customers, RCM works but it has to be implemented. Implementation takes time, so you must communicate progress. Communication and progress, more examples of leadership, structure and discipline!

As a RCM Facilitator or Practitioner, if you're looking to create a successful RCM effort at your company, you will need to communicate the progress of this effort on a regular basis. One fantastic way of communicating progress is to plan RCM Review meetings following the completion of each analysis. The objective of the RCM review meeting is to give your RCM team and area managers an opportunity to meet face to face. In thirty minutes, go through the RCM report and communicate the path forward to implement the tasks developed in the RCM analysis. The RCM team as well as local supervision and management should be invited to attend this meeting and I often ask the RCM team to lead the meeting.

The following items should be discussed/communicated at the RCM review meeting:

1. Present the systems covered in the RCM analysis.

2. Report the number of Functions, Functional Failures, Failure Modes and Tasks identified during the analysis.

3. Review the RCM Implementation Plan
   - Show how tasks were prioritized.
   - Show due dates for each priority.
   - Show a listing of who will be responsible for individual tasks.
   - Identify the RCM implementation manager and explain the role and responsibilities of the implementation manager.

4. Present significant findings from the RCM analysis. This could be new tasks developed or a significant failure mode identified in the analysis that could have resulted in a major failure or loss.

5. Take time to have the team express their thoughts about the RCM process. (Someone years ago told me this was risky because someone might say they hated the process! I continue asking and I and have yet to hear a bad word.)

6. Present the path forward now that the RCM analysis is complete. Show when you expect to complete the tasks and how implementation progress will be communicated.

Follow-Up Tasks
Tracking Results

The RCM Blitz™ Process Flow Model

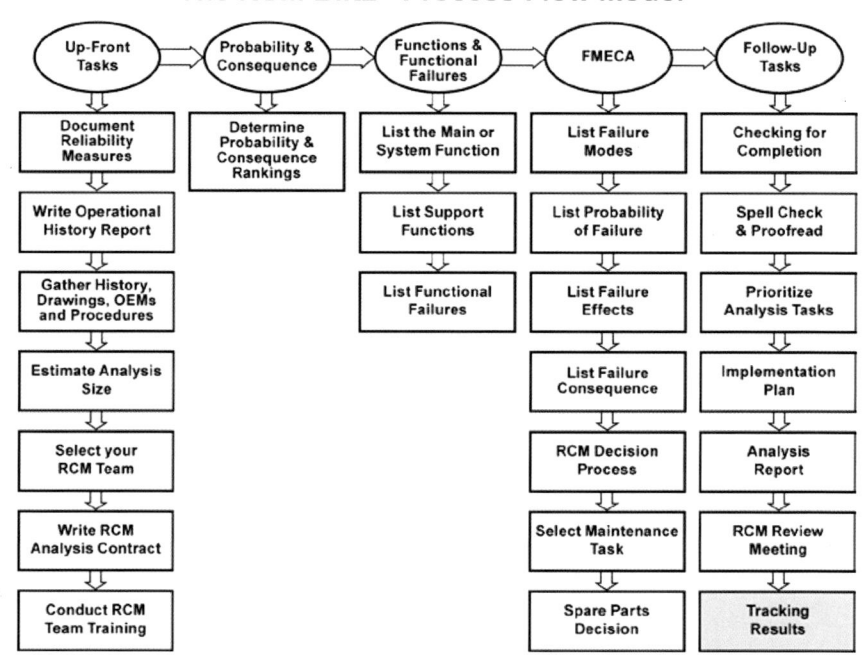

Up-Front Tasks	Probability & Consequence	Functions & Functional Failures	FMECA	Follow-Up Tasks
Document Reliability Measures	Determine Probability & Consequence Rankings	List the Main or System Function	List Failure Modes	Checking for Completion
Write Operational History Report		List Support Functions	List Probability of Failure	Spell Check & Proofread
Gather History, Drawings, OEMs and Procedures		List Functional Failures	List Failure Effects	Prioritize Analysis Tasks
Estimate Analysis Size			List Failure Consequence	Implementation Plan
Select your RCM Team			RCM Decision Process	Analysis Report
Write RCM Analysis Contract			Select Maintenance Task	RCM Review Meeting
Conduct RCM Team Training			Spare Parts Decision	Tracking Results

With over twelve years experience in instructing, mentoring and facilitating RCM analysis, I firmly believe that RCM is easy and it works. In my mind, the only reason a RCM effort fails at a plant is because people give up on the process. You don't need to be a CEO or upper level company director to make RCM Blitz™ work for your company, all you really need to do is follow the process and be driven to implement the tasks that come from your RCM team.

When it comes to Reliability Centered Maintenance, success is contagious. If you want RCM to become a part of your company culture all you need to do is ensure your first few RCM analyses are successful. Any time you can improve the reliability of a critical asset, lower the cost of maintenance, and reduce the unit cost of manufactured products, your managers and directors are going to want more and they are going to want more, now!

Lastly, I can not stress enough the importance of communication when it comes to implementation. If you are not communicating the progress of your implementation, you should assume that everyone involved is under the firm belief that NOTHING IS BEING DONE! When managers assume nothing is getting done, you are in danger of having your effort become history.

Tracking and reporting the results is the most important thing a facilitator and implementation manager can do. Show managers and team members what has been implemented on a regular basis (at least once each month) and continue to report the OEE of this asset as you work through getting items implemented and tasks completed.

Allied Reliability - RCM Blitz
Reliability Centered Maintenance Decision Flow Chart

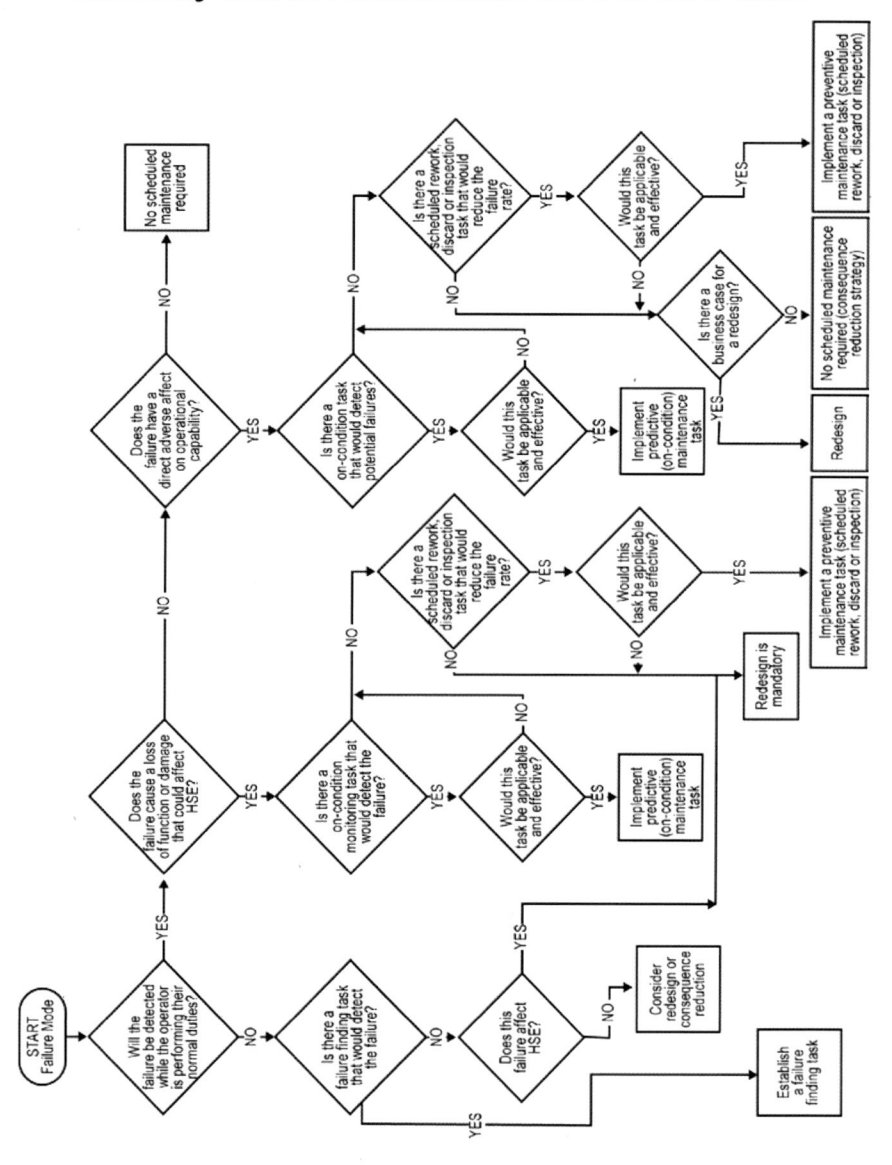

CHAPTER 7
General RCM Topics

Managing Your RCM Effort

After nearly thirty years it's no longer a secret that Reliability Centered Maintenance is a proven process that when properly applied will deliver a complete strategy for operating and maintaining your equipment that is designed to ensure the inherent designed reliability of your company's assets. In this chapter I will address a few successful models for putting in place a successful RCM effort that delivers not only thorough analyses, but a workable plan for implementing your analysis results. In getting started I think it's important to understand that while RCM is a process that requires leadership, structure, and discipline, while these three words might sound strict RCM also a process that can be molded to fit your company's culture and business model. My advice to managers who are looking to start a successful RCM effort is to closely review the four models listed below and then look for a company, practitioner and methodology that will work best to deliver your model.

RCM Model 1 - Practitioner/Expert Dependent RCM
The expert dependent RCM model is heavily dependent on an external, expert level RCM practitioner. Your RCM practitioner will work closely with a lead manager from your company to help select assets for analysis, schedule and perform each analysis, and work with your RCM.

RCM Model 1 - Pro's
I would have to say this is the easiest model to implement. This is why most consulting companies who offer RCM training and services try to sell this model. The expert practitioner brings the following benefits to your company:

- The experience of having performed over one hundred RCM analyses.
- A thorough understanding of the RCM process along with its potential benefits and pitfalls.
- They will ensure your RCM team covers nearly all potential failure modes.

- They will challenge not only your RCM team participants, but your company managers to ensure all failure modes are properly assessed (Companies training internal facilitators have found internal facilitators have a hard time challenging managers on difficult failure modes).
- They are driven to make sure your company has success with Reliability Centered Maintenance. Their livelihood and reputation depend on your success.
- This is typically the quickest way to complete the RCM cycle (Select Asset - Plan Analysis - Facilitate Analysis - Implement Analysis Results - Perform Tasks).
- They will bring with them real life experience on how to make RCM successful at your plant.

RCM Model 1 - Potential Problems
While there are several benefits to hiring a consultant/practitioner to head your RCM effort, this model can also have its problems. The list below outlines what I see as potential problems, along with a suggestion of how to keep this problem from derailing your effort.

- **Your RCM Practitioner is not really a RCM Expert** - I once reviewed a RCM analysis that was supposedly performed by a RCM practitioner/expert. In reviewing the document, it was clear this person had limited experience with RCM and little to no experience as a maintenance professional. I highly recommend that your company interview your RCM expert just like you were hiring this person as a new employee. Ask for specific examples of where they have applied RCM successfully along with the names of references you can call to verify they indeed have the credentials to drive your effort.

- **Your people have to believe in the expert and the RCM process** - This is the most common problem. Anytime you use an expert, you will find that people are reluctant to believe that, not only does this process work, but he/she knows how to make it work at your company. I can't tell you how many times I have heard the words, "I'm sure RCM works, but our company is different...". Each time I'm told this, I offer back that I love a challenge and I have yet to find a company that couldn't make RCM work. Start by listing your potential road blocks and work with your RCM team to develop a detailed plan on how "we are going to overcome these obstacles to make sure our first RCM is implemented."

- **Your RCM effort becomes expert dependent** - The problem with your RCM program becoming expert dependent is your progress in RCM will only progress as fast the expert's calendar will allow. When your expert leaves for a week or two, and people have questions regarding RCM or implementation, you have to wait for answers in order for things to progress forward. If your expert is busy training, facilitating and mentoring for other companies as well as yours, your progress may take longer as a result. The best RCM Practitioners are always busy, so if you're planning on going this route, I would set up fixed dates on the calendar as soon as possible.

RCM Model 2 - External Practitioner with Internal Facilitators

While this takes a little more time to develop than Model 1, once it is in place it will quickly pick up speed and in the end produce results faster than the first model. Model 2 uses an outside or consultant practitioner to train and mentor RCM facilitators who work for your company. The key task here is selecting the right people to become your RCM facilitators. This job requires some unique skill sets and as a result I would recommend your company take the time to set up a formal interview process for selecting RCM facilitators. To help you get started I created the following RCM Facilitator selection criteria.

Selecting Your RCM Facilitator

The people you select as your RCM facilitators will have a key role in the success of your RCM program. The RCM facilitators will have responsibilities in helping to select the equipment you choose to analyze, the depth or level of your analysis, who will participate in the analysis, as well as setting up and driving implementation of RCM tasks. The selection of your RCM facilitators is, in truth, more important than the selection of what equipment or process you analyze. In making this selection you should be looking for a person who meets the following criteria:

- *The RCM facilitator should be familiar with your process but need not be a process or equipment expert.* Experts too often bring with them bias on how the equipment should be operated or maintained.

- *The facilitator should have demonstrated the ability to work with some type of structured process that has lead to process or equipment improvement.* The RCM facilitator will be expected to facilitate a structured process, a series of questions that will lead a group to the correct level of maintenance. Good examples are SPC techniques, setting up corrective action guidelines, critical path planning or Root Cause Analysis.

- *The RCM facilitator should have demonstrated the ability to facilitate a structured meeting.* They will be expected to keep the RCM meetings on task and side conversations to a minimum. RCM is an in-depth, structured process that can often generate off-the-subject discussions. The job of the facilitator is to know how, and when, to bring the meeting back on track to keep the RCM process going at a steady pace. The facilitator will be expected to motivate the group in many different ways, bringing out input from shy people, while at the same time controlling more dominant personalities. *Leading RCM requires a person confident enough in the RCM process to challenge the bias of an engineer or technician.*

- *The RCM facilitator should have demonstrated the ability to be a leader while adhering to company values.* One of the most important jobs of facilitating RCM is knowing how to lead a group to consensus while ignoring your own bias. While facilitating RCM, they will be leading the group through a series of questions, in doing this, there is often the temptation to answer the questions for the group. It is important your facilitator understand and accept that their role in this process is to be the expert in RCM, while allowing the RCM team members to be the equipment experts.

- *The RCM facilitator needs to have demonstrated above-average computer skills.* A large part of the facilitator's job will be entering the analysis into a software package and preparing an analysis document. It is an expectation that your facilitator should be capable of entering this information into a software package, saving the information, and preparing a RCM document.

- *Print/Drawing Reading* - The facilitator must be able to read and interpret electrical, mechanical, and control drawings.

- *Background* - Reliability Engineer is most preferred, a highly skilled technical background with an expert level of understanding of the skilled trades. Must possess strong process skills (Process or Industrial Engineers). Strong people skills are a must.

RCM Model 2 - Pro's

- Your company RCM effort is no longer totally dependent on the expert practitioner.
- In developing internal RCM facilitators, you are creating a future RCM expert resource for your company.
- Your internal facilitators are well connected to your company and its goals. They have a thorough understanding of your critical assets, reliability measures, and where losses are occurring at your plant site.
- Internal facilitators can easily obtain up-front critical RCM information much easier than the external practitioner (drawings, procedures, OEM's).
- Internal facilitators are more aware of who the participants should be for each RCM analysis.

RCM Model 2 - Potential Problems

- **Selecting the wrong candidates as Facilitators** - This is the most common problem with RCM Model 2. To ensure you select the correct people as your RCM facilitators, I suggest you closely follow the facilitator selection criteria listed in this chapter and have the external Practitioner/Expert be part of your interviewing process.

- **Your internal facilitators don't have enough experience to influence change** - Creating a RCM culture at your facility requires time, success and experience, in that specific order. Time to train people, select assets, perform analyses, implement analysis results and perform tasks. Companies that have leadership, structure and discipline can accomplish this cycle in two months the first time, and in one month for the remainder of their analyses. Success comes from selecting the correct assets and implementing the tasks, if you do both, your RCM's will be successful. Experience comes from completing this cycle, over and over again, with solid results and this can only take place with strong leadership.

- **Overloading your internal facilitators** - This problem ranks nearly as high as selecting the wrong candidate. The problem develops when a company selects good people and then overloads their schedules with five other things along with RCM. My suggestion to companies is to make the lead facilitator a full time job. As the individuals learn and grow, add some additional responsibilities as they become comfortable with their RCM facilitator roles and responsibilities.

RCM Model 3 – Development of Internal RCM Practitioner/Expert

When implemented properly, Model 3 should follow Model 2. In other words, your company should first look to train and develop facilitators, and from that group of certified facilitators, select one or two people to develop as RCM Practitioners. Your RCM practitioners will then take on the lead role for your company RCM effort developing a plan for roll out of RCM, training, mentoring and certification of future RCM facilitators. While I would rank this as the most desired model, I would also note that this takes time and dedication. I would recommend that a facilitator have at least 10 RCM analyses completed and implemented prior to becoming trained as a practitioner. Reliability Centered Maintenance is a tedious process. It requires a load of patience and even more discipline to become a practitioner, in the end you have to love the process to become a RCM practitioner.

RCM Model 3 - Pro's

Model 3 contains all the Pro's of Model 2 plus the following:

- This is the most cost effective way to create a RCM culture at your company.
- Your internal expert, if properly trained, will have a world of experience in RCM, making it easy to identify assets for analysis, perform the analyses, implement the results, and report the results of each success.
- Your internal practitioner will be a resource for the rest of your company when it comes to Reliability Centered Maintenance and Manufacturing Reliability.

RCM Model 3 - Potential Problems

- **Training practitioners too early** - I am fully aware of some companies that sell RCM training services that will sign up anyone who expresses the desire to become a RCM practitioner with no experience in performing RCM. I can tell you in all honesty that you cannot create a RCM practitioner with 1 month of classroom training. The experience in actually facilitating several RCM analyses on various types of equipment best qualifies one to attend practitioner certification. Rushing this process might deliver a person who academically understands Reliability Centered Maintenance but has no life experience in actually facilitating the process and implementing the results. Fast Track Practitioner training is very expensive and has a very poor success rate. If you want an internal Practitioner, take my advice and make sure this person is actually capable of facilitating the process, implementing the tasks and showing proven results before investing in practitioner training.

- **You train your Practitioner and then they leave your company** - People who are certified RCM practitioners contain a skill set that companies all over the world are in need of. If you don't believe me, go to SMRP.org or ReliabilityWeb.com and take a look at all the companies who are looking for people with RCM experience. If you plan on training a RCM practitioner be prepared to match, or best, benefits packages offered by other companies in your area.

RCM Model 4 - The Self Trained RCM Expert
As I began writing this chapter, I decided to call an old friend who is also a RCM practitioner to see what he thought about the four models. His advice was to leave the last one out as, "it rarely works and when it does, they usually make so many mistakes that other people in this company no longer believe in the viability of RCM as a reliability tool." While his advice is true, I have decided to include the Self-Trained Expert as Model 4. I made this decision from working with a few small yet proactive manufacturing companies. Small companies have little to spend when it comes to training, and while this is true, they still have a strong desire to improve reliability and cut costs. As a result, their people will begin searching the internet for ideas on how to cut costs and improve reliability. In this search, they find tools like Root Cause Analysis, Cause Mapping, RCM Blitz™ and so on. As they begin reading about these tools, and the results that companies achieve through training, performing and implementing RCM, they make the call to inquire about training. The first question they ask is how much does this cost? OUCH!

For those people who want to learn about RCM on their own, there is plenty of information available on the web. I, myself, would start with the original RCM document published by Stan Nowlan and Howard Heap. This huge document can be obtained on the web for free and while it was first published in 1978, it truly is the basis from which all good RCM methodologies were founded. Once you have finished, I would recommend you begin to outline the seven steps of RCM and how you plan to go about completing these steps. To do this, I would use this book, or a couple of others written by Mac Smith and John Moubray, as resources.

When you're ready to get started, don't be afraid to develop a phone or e-mail relationship with a certified RCM practitioner. Anyone in this business who is worth the dirt they walk on would be more than willing to give you a few minutes here and there for coaching, and if you're looking for a mentor, simply page through a few conference presentations for a list of names.

RCM Model 4 - Pro's

- It's cheap!
- It's quite satisfying to learn on your own.
- Understanding and performing RCM makes people marketable.

RCM Model 4 - Potential Problems (This list could be huge, I kept it to the obvious)

- **Time** - Be prepared for this to take well over a year before you learn enough to become confident with the process.

- **Mistakes** - Your first several RCM analyses will be loaded with mistakes. You have to hope that none are severe enough to derail your effort.

- **Support** - Because you are learning, you will be tempted to change the process. Others who don't know the process will also encourage you to make changes. As a result, your attempts to start may fail over and over again, and before long you give up. My suggestion is start with Nowlan and Heap, stick to that for your first few analyses and make changes one at a time.

When and How to Template A RCM Analysis

RCM Blitz™ is a Reliability Tool designed to develop a complete maintenance strategy for a process or piece of equipment. When implemented, this maintenance strategy will help to ensure the inherent designed reliability of any process or asset. Performing an RCM analysis takes an investment in time and resources to complete, so I always advise my clients to follow the RCM Blitz™ process to ensure the equipment they have selected to analyze will show a return on their investment dollars.

Typically, while performing the first or second analysis in a given company, I am questioned about the feasibility of copying the information from one analysis and pasting it into another. "This will save both time and money and should provide an equal level of reliability across all of our assets." This idea of developing a maintenance strategy for one asset, and applying it to similar assets, seems very attractive, but it's also often the first crucial mistake companies make when trying to start a RCM program. Common sense leads them to assume a pump is a pump, a motor is a motor and pipe is pipe. If we expect our pumps, motors and pipes to perform similar duties, they should in turn deliver similar levels of reliability. In the rush to make the RCM cycle faster, they forget to consider just how different these identical components can be. In the end, they discover that the maintenance strategy that works well for one asset will not work at all for another. Worse, they might believe it was the RCM process that failed and tell others, "We tried RCM and it didn't work!"

Common Ways People Attempt to Template RCM and the Problems Associated with Each

1. In making the decision to develop RCM Templates, a common high level maintenance strategy is developed for common assets such as pumps, motors and gearboxes. The assumption is made for instance, that all centrifugal pumps should be lubricated on the same schedule, and that vibration analysis should be performed on each pump on a monthly basis. In doing this, the CMMS becomes populated with PM and PdM tasks based on this same assumption without ever considering asset criticality.

    Problems with this strategy
    - The problem with making the assumption that a pump is a pump, a motor is a motor, a gearbox is a gearbox, and we should be able to maintain them all the same way and get similar results, is that this is rarely true. Identical assets can have very different failure modes depending on the service, duty and environment they are being operated in. Add to these, differences in design and installation practices, and we now have two "identical" assets with very different levels of reliability.

    - This attempt at building PM and PdM templates fills your CMMS with maintenance tasks that may have no effect on asset reliability. In many cases these tasks could decrease the reliability of the asset.

2. They perform a RCM analysis on one manufacturing asset and make the assumption that they can transfer the tasks from the first RCM to other like assets.

   Problems with this strategy
   - While it is possible to use the maintenance tasks determined in one RCM analysis on similar assets, doing so without considering the failure modes of the second will not produce identical levels of reliability. Similar to the first example, making the assumption that the assets are truly identical can be a big mistake. While many assets look alike, they can be very different when it comes to instruments, controls and programming.

   - I often see companies attempt to use this strategy from plant to plant and this rarely works. Operating environment, plant condition, design, installation and programming changes make assets very different from one plant to the next.

3. Purchasing completed RCM analyses for common assets or systems.

   Problems with this strategy
   - This attempt at RCM templates is the worst. I have yet to see a completed RCM for sale that even closely represented the asset as it existed at the plant site. RCM will not deliver results unless the failure modes identified, and the tasks identified to mitigate each failure mode, represent the actual asset and supporting components installed at your plant.

Can you ever template information from one RCM analysis and use it in another?

Yes, it can be done and it can save both time and money, but there are several things that need to be considered before you copy the maintenance strategy from one analysis and paste it into another. Reliability-Centered Maintenance is a relatively simple process with several subtle complexities that lulls people into making common mistakes.

In order to template information from one RCM analysis to another, you need to follow and meet all of these guidelines:

1. **The assets you intend to template must be identical in make, manufacture, material and how they are operated.**

   Example - Your company is performing a RCM analysis on a cooling water pump. The company has three similar cooling water systems at this plant site. Before you template the information from the first analysis to the other systems, make sure that all three pumps are the same make, manufacturer, model and material. This is important. Different brands, types and materials may have different failure modes and different rates of failure. On top of this, the operating context or operating requirements for the systems may also be different and may also result in differing failure modes and failure rates. Are the pumps required to pump identical rates of cooling water at identical pressures? Is the water in one system treated with a chemical that's different from the others? Take some time to look at requirements of all three systems and try to determine where each is different, and what failures may result from these differences.

2. **Assets where you intend to template information from one analysis to another should be identical in operating environment.**

   Example - Using the cooling water systems we described above, imagine the plant is located in Minnesota. One of the systems is outside, while the other two are inside. Knowing this, might we have some different failure modes that require different levels of maintenance? The Operating Environment of our assets also includes the age of the assets and the condition of surrounding or supporting assets.

   While our first system is located outside, it has only been in service for five years, the pump itself is mounted on a manufacturer's base, and the pump base is grouted and supported by a large concrete foundation. The pump on our third system has been in service for twelve years and is bolted to the building floor. What are the chances that these two identical pumps have identical failure modes and failure rates? If I performed identical levels of maintenance on these pumps would they deliver identical levels of reliability? Of course not!

3. **If you intend to template information from one RCM analysis to another, remember to consider the specific failure modes for each location.**

Example - Getting to the specific cause of failure is a major key in performing successful RCM analyses. There is a common tendency when starting Reliability-Centered Maintenance to begin writing failure modes at a specific cause level and then gradually move to higher levels of failure. This always results in an ineffective "one size fits all" maintenance strategy. This does not work if you are looking to achieve the inherent designed level of reliability for your assets. It never has and it never will. Looking back to the cooling tower pumps, if we started our company RCM program looking at the first outdoor system and discussed this pump's failures at specific cause level, the product of our RCM analysis would be a complete maintenance strategy that addresses the specific failure modes of the asset. The implemented maintenance strategy from this RCM analysis would ensure a high level of reliability for this asset. Now, to save some money we try to apply this same maintenance strategy to our second or third system. Would this maintenance strategy now deliver the same level of reliability for these assets? Not a chance! The maintenance strategy developed in the first analysis most likely would never address some of the specific failure modes that directly affect the reliability of the other systems.

When attempting to template RCM information between like assets you should **ALWAYS** remember to consider the specific failure modes of each asset no matter how much alike they first appear. The best way to do this is:

- Make sure you are using a cross-functional RCM team that is made up of experts who work with, and are responsible for, the maintenance of each asset. They are the only people who will know the specific causes of failure for your assets.
- As a general rule, it should take you 1/5 the time to complete a good RCM template. This includes gathering information and history on each system, and performing the analysis.
- Remember, there may be some failures and tasks applied to the first asset that may not apply to your next. It is also possible to perform unnecessary maintenance.
- Common, specific, cause failure mode lists can be helpful to ensure all likely failures are considered.

How to Perform RCM in a Reactive Maintenance Culture
As I work with manufacturing clients who have made the decision to train and mentor RCM facilitators, I often hear these words, "This RCM stuff is real good, it makes so much sense, but it won't work here. Our management likes to spend money on things like this so they can say,

"We tried RCM" but they won't support implementing or performing the identified tasks". And just as often I hear, "You don't understand, maintenance brought you in here. The managers in operations don't believe in this stuff and won't support it. Operation's owns the equipment and they pay us to fix it. They don't want to be told by us when the machine can run and when it needs to be down. This stuff is good but we don't have a chance."

Welcome to the world of reactive maintenance! This is a world full of excuses from both sides of the business table, operations and maintenance. (Most common excuse; "We're not ready for RCM. Is there something easier we can do first?") A world that makes business exciting, reactive maintenance makes your blood pump and it's full of wonderful highs and dreadful lows. This is a world full of recognition for saving the day and putting out the fire, and blame for taking a risk that resulted in a failure.

So, how can you implement an RCM Culture in a business where a reactive maintenance culture has been a way of life for several years? I am asked this question several times a year and I always give the same reply, "It's difficult but not impossible. The speed and acceptance of changing from a reactive maintenance culture to a RCM culture depends on your level of resolve and discipline." Resolve is a measure of how much you want to change. How strongly do you feel about reactive maintenance being the wrong way to perform maintenance? Discipline is your willingness to measure how much this reactive maintenance culture is costing your business and presenting this information to operations managers. Resolve and discipline can be a stretch for us maintenance people. We generally don't like to admit it, but a lot of us happen to like this Reactive Maintenance Culture. It brings us heaps of attention, both positive and negative. Our skilled-trades people are continuously reinforced in this culture, both emotionally and financially. They are told over and over how important they are to the business because they can fix things quickly and make us run again. They are financially reinforced through the overtime that comes with a maintenance culture. In spite of liking the attention that comes with this Reactive Maintenance Culture, the reality of its downside sets in when, as a maintenance supervisor or maintenance manager, you are asked, year after year, to reduce the costs of the maintenance budget. Where will you get this money? Your culture requires loads of spare parts and lots of people to replace them. If you remove some parts from your inventory and those parts fail, you will take the blame when the machine is down while waiting for parts. Remove some people to save money and you only increase the stress and overtime for your existing people. You're in a catch twenty-two. How can you possibly reduce maintenance costs in this environment? Reliability Centered Maintenance can bring maintenance costs under control and make your equipment more reliable. To make RCM happen in this culture you must have a plan.

Planning a Successful RCM Effort

Step 1 – Measure

In order to make this culture shift, you must have buy-in from both operations and maintenance. This can only be accomplished with real data. You will have to show what the reactive maintenance culture is costing the business. The best way to show this cost is through reliability measures. Overall Equipment Effectiveness (OEE) and Total Effective Equipment Performance (TEEP) measured in terms of good product manufactured versus key manufacturing losses will clearly show the effects of a reactive maintenance culture. Setting up and performing these measures also accomplishes two important things: it helps to clearly identify the correct piece of equipment to perform a RCM analysis on and it sets up a baseline to show the successful results of your RCM effort. Publish the report and display your monthly maintenance costs. Maintenance costs in a reliable business should be predictable and steady. It is highly important in the early stages of this transition to show how out of control and unpredictable your costs have become. Publish the report and display the percent of time your people spend on Emergency Demand Maintenance, Planned and Scheduled Corrective Maintenance, and Predictive/Preventive Maintenance. Maintenance planning and scheduling of corrective and predictive/preventive maintenance in a reliable business is easy because it is predictable.

Step 2 – Plan and Educate

Educating people in why you need to make the shift from a Reactive Maintenance Culture to a Reliability Centered Culture is an important step that many people tend to skip. The general tendency here is to bring in the consultant and let him or her explain why RCM is important, how it works, and why they should want to do it. The problem with this plan is the consultant is only on board with your company for a short time. While the consultant is on-site your people will believe and participate but as soon as they leave their belief quickly fades. **You,** as a maintenance or operations manager, need to prepare your people for this transition. **You** need to begin demonstrating your resolve to make this change to your people. Do this by involving your people in every step of the process, from the measures to the celebration.

Start with developing a **realistic** plan to select a piece of equipment to perform a Reliability Centered Maintenance Analysis on (remember this selection should be identified by measuring OEE & TEEP). This plan should clearly show **who** will be trained as RCM Facilitators, **who** will be trained as RCM Participants, **when** and **where** the analysis will take place, **who** will be responsible to ensure the tasks from this analysis will be implemented and **when** they will be completed (In most cases I suggest that **you** be responsible for the implementation of the first couple of analyses). The plan should show **who** is going to be responsible for performing your identified Predictive, Preventive and Failure-Finding tasks and if you presently have the skill base to perform these tasks. Should gaps in these capabilities be found, you will need to create a plan to educate people to close these gaps.

This is also a good time to do some benchmarking with other companies who have an existing Reliability Centered Maintenance Culture. The purpose of this is two-fold, first to get an idea of the consultant you may want to use for training, and second, to get a realistic idea of how long this culture shift will take.

Step 3 – Train

Training people in how to perform a thorough RCM analysis will require a skilled consultant. Do yourself a big favor and take some time to do this step right. Research several firms that provide traditional RCM Training and Facilitation services. (It is important that you use a traditional form of RCM. There are several short-cut RCM methods available, each created for companies who do not have the discipline or resolve to make the culture shift traditional RCM provides.) The objective of Reliability Centered Maintenance is to develop a complete maintenance strategy that consists of the following:

- **Predictive Maintenance Tasks**
- **Preventive Maintenance Tasks**
- **Failure-Finding Tasks**
- **Redesign Recommendations**
- **Consequence Reduction Tasks (Tasks recommended to reduce Mean Time To Restore (MTTR) for failures that**

cannot be predicted, prevented, or eliminated through redesign)
- **Spare Parts Recommendations**

Ask each of these companies to provide references for successful RCM implementations. Check out these references to be sure the company has the training, has performed several analyses, has implemented the analysis tasks and can show results from their efforts. While performing this research, you should not only be looking for a specific RCM process but a specific consultant. The consultant you choose should have a high success rate, not only at training facilitators in the RCM process, but also at training them well enough that the company is able to make the culture shift. Several companies may offer RCM services, but there are only a few people who know the application, or RCM, well enough to help you make this change. This person should have extensive experience not only in instructing RCM, but also in performing analyses across several types of businesses. Once you have identified your RCM process and consultant, you can now select your RCM facilitators and schedule the training.

Your RCM facilitators should be selected from some of the best employees your company has to offer. While I am often asked to provide a profile for what qualifications an RCM facilitator should have, I still, on occasion, arrive to provide training only to find a person not suited to lead a line to the cafeteria, let alone a RCM analysis. Your facilitators should have demonstrated the following qualities:

- **A high level of understanding of the skilled trades**
- **The ability to troubleshoot and identify failures at root cause level**
- **A thorough understanding of good proactive maintenance practices such as laser alignment, and the importance of proper torque specifications**
- **The ability to write a step-by-step detailed and measurable preventive maintenance procedure**
- **They are highly respected among their peers**
- **The ability to lead a team through a structured process or meeting and maintain control and schedule**
- **A good to high level knowledge of computers and databases**
- **A natural drive to accomplish difficult tasks**
- **The ability to develop a detailed plan to implement and track analysis tasks**

Following this list of required qualities, I will now add that your facilitators do not need to be degreed Engineers or Technicians. I have trained highly successful RCM facilitators that were Trades-People, Operators, Mechanical and Electrical Technicians, Industrial Engineers, Mechanical Engineers and Chemical Engineers. Most important is to be sure the person is comfortable, qualified and has the natural drive to help make this change successful.

Your RCM training should be held in a large comfortable room, and if possible, dedicated just to RCM training and analyses. When scheduling your RCM facilitator training, plan on training your participants and beginning your first analysis the very next week. The training will be fresh in their minds and they will be excited to start this first analysis.

Step 4 - Perform

With your facilitators and participants trained, you can now begin your first RCM analysis. This first RCM analysis should be kicked off by **you,** the RCM sponsor. The team will have been trained in the RCM process but it is important that you reinforce why you are about to begin performing RCM analyses to determine your maintenance strategy. Let the team know that you are aware that this process takes time and dedication. Remember, you are still living in a reactive culture and the people about to begin this analysis will still be feeling the draw to show their importance by being called out of the analysis to fight a fire. People will often ask me, "How can we spend this much time talking about this piece of equipment?" The best response is hard data; show them how much time was spent repairing the equipment due to unplanned failures and what it cost the company for that downtime. When you have finished your kick-off, stay with the team for an hour or so and just observe. From here, it's your consultant's job to lead your effort, keep your facilitators and team on schedule, and finish the analysis on or ahead of time. Stop in each day for lunch to answer questions and offer support. Remember the importance of verbal positive reinforcement. It's important your team hears that you support this effort and their recommendations.

Through this first analysis and the next few analyses where your facilitators are mentored, it is important you set up regular communication meetings with your consultant. Set aside fifteen to twenty minutes each day to meet with your consultant and discuss the progress of the facilitators and the team. A good consultant will provide written progress reports on each facilitator along with suggestions on where this person needs to improve.

Step 5 – Report

With this first analysis completed, it is now time to develop your implementation plan and print the analysis results out in report form. Schedule a one-hour meeting to communicate the findings of the RCM team. Show the analysis report and implementation plan. Provide a summary of the analysis findings, including the number of failure modes covered, the number of predictive, preventive, failure-finding, and redesign tasks. Communicate who will be responsible for implementing the tasks that came out of your analysis and when you plan on completing this implementation. Show the plan for your path forward including when you will begin performing the implemented tasks, how you will provide the resources to perform these tasks and a schedule for communication meetings to update people on RCM progress.

Remember, communicating the progress of your RCM effort is important in reinforcing that RCM will become the way you perform maintenance. Skipping these meetings sends the message that this effort is not important to you.

Step 6 – Audit and Track Results

Identifying the correct maintenance tasks by performing an RCM analysis and implementing those tasks into your CMMS only completes two-thirds of the RCM cycle. Actually performing the tasks completes the cycle. To ensure this final step of the process is being completed at regular intervals, you will need to set up regular RCM audits. You will need to set aside time to perform random audits of new maintenance tasks. The purpose of these audits is three-fold; it will reinforce that you are serious about making the shift to a RCM culture, provide you with an opportunity to reinforce the people who are performing the tasks correctly and on schedule, and provide a means to learn and modify your effort as new knowledge is developed. Don't make the assumption that because you now have RCM maintenance tasks set up within you CMMS and people are charging time to them that they are in fact being completed. Remember your people have been recognized and reinforced for years for fixing things that were broken, for getting operations up and running again. They will need to be thanked just as often for completing your RCM tasks and reminded of their importance to the business.

Tracking your RCM results should be communicated at your regular communication meetings referred to in Step 4. You will need to show how much of your first analysis has been implemented, how many of these tasks are now being completed on a regular basis (Audit compliance), your monthly maintenance costs, and most important, the OEE and TEEP measures for the asset you performed the analysis on. Data proving a successful RCM analysis breeds acceptance, excitement and a willingness to make this culture shift actually happen. Report and celebrate this accomplishment, acknowledge everyone who had a hand in making this success happen, RCM Facilitators, Analysis Participants, Planners, Trades-People and Operators for performing the tasks, and managers and supervisors for making people available for training, analyses, and tasks.

Keeping Your Effort Going

Keeping your RCM effort going should be easy once you have achieved your first success. In fact, you will have to avoid the common temptation of moving too fast. RCM done well can be like a snowball rolling downhill, building in size, momentum, and speed until it becomes uncontrollable and crashes. Take my advice, moving to an RCM culture should not be a race. Too often, companies get excited after the first analysis. They then set an aggressive schedule to perform one analysis after another, and often several at the same time. When it comes time to implement the tasks from these analyses, they are not prepared to dedicate the resources needed for implementation and the program crashes. Again, RCM should not be a race. Complete your first analysis, implement the tasks and then begin your next analysis. A good general rule of thumb, once you have proven that RCM works, is to schedule the next analysis to start when 80% of the tasks from the previous analysis have been completed. Slow and steady wins this race. Results and direct savings are best achieved by taking the time to identify your next asset for analysis by using your reliability measures from Step One. Again, demonstrate that you are using a process with real data to determine what to analyze next, not emotion. In doing this, you cement the learning from your RCM training and you show your commitment to doing things the right way.

In closing, it's important to remember that Reliability Centered Maintenance is a powerful reliability tool with a proven track record. It takes training, time, and repetition to become comfortable with the process and dozens of analyses to build your knowledge level to that of an expert. Working closely with your consultant is the best way to shorten this learning curve. It's a good idea to set up some regular communication with your consultant (a good one who truly cares about your effort won't charge for a phone call) and have your analyses reviewed for content and accuracy. The more you learn and apply RCM, the more reliable your business will become. Once this becomes your culture, your people will become proactive thinkers providing career lasting benefits to your business.

CHAPTER 8
Scoring Your RCM Effort

In the early years of providing RCM Blitz™ services for companies I was often challenged in regard to the validity of the RCM Blitz™ process and my experience as a RCM facilitator. I always felt the best way to answer these questions was to provide information that detailed a clear record of success.

We take time to ensure we analyze equipment that will provide a return on investment, we put in place a detailed implementation plan and we hold people accountable to complete the implementation.

When it comes to Reliability Centered Maintenance, the world has hundreds of people who can talk a lot about RCM. About half of these people who talk about RCM have actually been able to complete a RCM analysis and I would guess that less than 25 percent of these people have implemented the tasks from their completed analysis. Now ask yourself the question, if the asset they performed and implemented was not a critical asset, did it provide a return on investment?

Not likely!

Now, if you spent nearly thirty thousand dollars of company money on a project that lasted months on end and were not able to show a return on investment, would your manager then say "Let's do more of this!"

Not a chance!

When it comes to RCM Blitz™ we made the decision from day 1 to provide a SAE compliant methodology that will be completed quickly, includes a way to assign and track implementation and will provide a clear return on investment.

When it comes to RCM, winners keep score and the others....well they move on and try something else!

Like it or not we live in a society that likes to keep score. The score provides feedback; it gives those who are not involved information on the progress or success of those who are involved. The score can be delivered in an endless number of formats: the price of your company stock, net profits, unit cost of product, overall equipment effectiveness, or percent emergency/demand maintenance. In the world of Reliability Centered Maintenance, Terry O'Hanlon gathered a team of experts including Jack Nicholas and myself several years ago to develop the RCM Scorecard. The result of this effort was a comprehensive tool that evaluated Key Performance Indicators at various periods before and during an RCM Project. I have to say I was grateful for being involved with this effort as the finished product resulted in a tool that would deliver remarkable feedback on the maturity of an ongoing RCM effort. If you want detailed information on the progress of your RCM effort, the RCM Scorecard would provide that information. In addition to this, the scorecard also provided the option to be flexible and simple. Anyone who knows Jack understands while he is thorough in his work he has a genuine appreciation for simplicity. The quest to make RCM simple is what made Jack and I friends and nearly ten years after working with Jack on the RCM Scorecard I have decided to write an article in regard to how to score your RCM effort using a few simple yet easy to answer questions. The result is a simple and quick method that will allow one to judge the potential success of their effort as well as identify areas where more coaching and mentoring are needed.

Using the original Scorecard as a template we can view your ongoing RCM effort in four phases:

1. **Baseline Metrics** - (How are you selecting assets for analysis?)
2. **Analysis Phase Metrics** - (Are we following the RCM process?)
3. **Implementation Phase Metrics** - (How are we doing at implementing RCM tasks?)
4. **Benefits Phase Metrics** - (Are we seeing benefits from our new RCM maintenance strategy?)

BaselineMetrics
Starting with the Baseline Metrics let's cut to the chase and begin this simplification by stating that RCM is not a tool that needs to be used on every asset at your facility. Reliability Centered Maintenance is a tool that will provide a return on investment provided we direct is use to critical assets and assets with poor reliability performance measures. Simplification in my mind also results in asking closed factual questions whenever possible. Closed factual questions elicit *yes* or *no* answers, we either use a formal process to select assets for RCM analyses or we don't. In my mind answers like *sometimes*, *maybe* or *on occasion* open the door for bull, and when bull enters the conversation the truth often walks out.

Baseline Metric Questions

1. Is the asset selected for RCM analysis in the top 5 to 20 percent of your critical assets? If the answer is yes score 1 point, if the answer is no or you have not performed an asset criticality assessment the score is zero. If you have not performed a formal asset criticality assessment I would highly recommend you do so.

2. Are we measuring OEE for the selected asset? Score 1 point if the answer is yes, zero if the answer is no. Overall Equipment Effectiveness will be one way to determine the success of your RCM strategy. If you are not measuring OEE on critical assets I would recommend that you start doing so.

3. Is the selected asset suffering from equipment based failures in any of the following Key Manufacturing Losses: Operational Losses, Speed Losses, Quality Losses? Score 1 point for a yes answer, zero for a no answer. The key manufacturing losses are a function of Overall Equipment Effectiveness losses resulting from equipment based failures are a good indication of a poor maintenance strategy.

4. Is the percent Emergency/Demand maintenance performed on this asset greater than 25%? Score 1 for a yes answer and zero for a no answer. A high amount of emergency and demand maintenance is a good indicator of poor maintenance practices.

Evaluation of Baseline Metric Questions
A score of 3 or 4 out of 4 delivers an excellent candidate for RCM analysis. A score of 2 out of 4 or lower is a good indication that we need to select another asset for analysis.

Analysis Phase Metrics
Analysis Phase Metrics give us a snapshot view of two key items:

- Did our facilitators do a good job in completing our Up-Front tasks? This includes RCM estimates, gathering of information, team training and RCM Facilitation.
- Did we follow the RCM process in completing this analysis?

Analysis Phase Questions

1. Was the analysis time estimate within 10% of the actual time spent to perform the analysis? Score 1 for yes, zero for no. Good facilitators know how to keep the team focused to complete each analysis on time. Finishing too early may be a sign that several failure modes may have been missed or written at a high level. The ability to accurately estimate the time it will take a team to perform a RCM analysis is dependent on the number of Functions and Failure Modes analyzed. Time is money, we ask for your best people when we perform a RCM analysis and we want to utilize this time to bring benefit to your business.

2. Are Failure Modes being written in a three part format? (Part, Problem, Specific Cause) Score 1 for yes and zero for no. I want to point out that answers like sometimes or most of the time does not count here. Good RCM facilitators understand the importance of writing good failure modes all the time.

3. Are the tasks identified applicable and effective in mitigating each failure mode? Score 1 for yes and zero for no. I have to say that the person evaluating this question should have a thorough understanding of RCM. I see hundreds of examples of what some people believe are good analyses, in the end if the task mitigates the failure mode, we have wasted our time.

4. Did the RCM Facilitator work with the team to identify all the hidden failures and resulting failure finding tasks for this asset? Score 1 for yes and zero for no. Again as stated along with question 3 you will need a person with a thorough understanding of RCM to report an accurate answer to this question. Accurate assessment of hidden failures is a critical component of a first class RCM effort.

Evaluation of Analysis Phase Metrics
A score of 3 out of 4 or better is outstanding! The analysis phase of Reliability Centered Maintenance is extremely important. It sets the stage for a successful RCM outcome and if we cut corners here our results will suffer.

A score of 2 out of 4 or less is a good indication that your RCM facilitator is in need of more mentoring or coaching. Chances are if you're scoring in this range, you are wasting both time and money.

While I have seen a few people get lucky and post some huge results on a few well analyzed failure modes the odds are against continued success.

Implementation Phase Metrics

I have always loved the phrase "Implementation is the graveyard of RCM". The phrase clearly describes the importance of good planning and follow through when it comes to implementing the task recommendations from each RCM analysis. As we train RCM Facilitators we try to make it very clear that unless we implement the tasks discovered in the analysis phase we have simply wasted a bunch of money talking about what is likely to happen to our equipment. Implementation is where the work really begins. We now have to take the recommendations of the RCM team and make them an ongoing part of how we now plan to manage this critical asset.

Implementation Phase Questions

1. Have we named a specific individual as the RCM Implementation Manager? Score 1 for yes, zero for no. When I say name I mean a person's name and not a title.

2. Has each RCM Task been assigned a priority, due date and responsible person? Score 1 for yes, zero for no. Just like the implementation manager I want names assigned to each RCM task along with due dates that match the task priority. Implementing the RCM tasks is simple project management and we need to hold people accountable for implementing their assigned tasks.

3. Is the RCM Implementation Manager communicating implementation progress that includes percent of tasks implemented and implementation schedule compliance? Score 1 for yes, zero for no. We need to know the leaders and laggards in our organization, leaders need to be reinforced and laggards may need more coaching or resources.

4. Are we implementing at least 80% of our RCM task recommendations? Score 1 for yes, zero for no. If we are implementing more that's great but if it's less than eighty percent I would begin to worry that we may be cherry picking the results of each analysis. Picking the low hanging fruit can produce results but doing this is a gamble that many times results in temporary benefits. A complete maintenance strategy that ensures the designed reliability of your asset will only come from implementing all the tasks identified by the RCM team.

Evaluation of Implementation Phase Questions
Score 3 out of 4 you are doing a good job, 4 out of 4 and you can start planning a celebration. You are now managing and implementing the tasks from your RCM analysis and in completing this phase of RCM you will soon see results. Start planning your next RCM analysis because you have proven that you can implement!

Score 2 out of 4 or worse and you had better put the brakes on your effort and start holding people accountable. At this point you have everything you need to make the effort a success but are not willing to do the work to make it happen. As a seasoned RCM practitioner nothing pains me more than to see a fantastic RCM analysis sit on a shelf advertising the money wasted for what could have been! Don't you dare plan another analysis at this point.

Benefits Phase Metrics
Regardless of the score in all other areas, don't kid yourself, this is where your RCM effort will be judged. This being said, if you scored high in the first three categories you are very likely to have a high score here as well.

Benefits Phase Questions

1. Are the implemented RCM tasks now part of the regular routine maintenance and operating schedule for this equipment? Score 1 for yes and zero for no. In order to see any benefit from your RCM implementation we must now make these tasks part of our routine schedule.

2. Are 90% of the scheduled RCM tasks being completed as part of our routine schedule? Score 1 for yes, zero for no. Completing these tasks will now ensure the benefit of reliability. Failing to complete them will result in a return to our old habits.

3. Has Overall Equipment Effectiveness (OEE) for this asset improved by more than 10 percent? Score 1 for yes and zero for no. I have seen way more than 10% but this figure will provide the return on investment needed to keep your RCM effort going.

4. **Has the amount of Emergency and Demand maintenance been reduced by more than 10 percent?** Score 1 for yes and zero for no. Reducing the amount of emergency and demand maintenance will have a direct impact on maintenance costs as well as efficiency.

Evaluating Benefits Phase Metrics
Score 4 out of 4 and your group has hit a home run! Chances are we now have a long list of assets we want to perform RCM on.

Score 3 out of 4 and we have done well. In most cases we failed question number 2 and we need to then work to improve on scheduling and completing tasks. It is important to recognize a failing score on number 2 will always impact the result of questions 3 and 4.

A score of 2 or less out of 4 shows that we elected to try and hit but failed to swing the bat! Put some work into questions 1 and 2 and the results of 3 and 4 are sure to follow. If we scored high in the first three phases and low on the last phase it's because we have not followed through at completing the tasks. At this point we need to ensure operations and maintenance are working together to complete the RCM tasks.

In closing I again want to stress that this is a simple but very effective RCM Scorecard. If one wanted to perform a very thorough assessment of their effort, the RCM Scorecard created by our team can be found at reliabilityweb.com.

CLOSING

Well, the world now has another book about Reliability Centered Maintenance. My goal in writing this book was to make clear how to properly perform a RCM Blitz™ analysis. For years now, I have had certified facilitators and practitioners asking me to send them anything I have written in regards to the Blitz methodology. The goal I really wanted to achieve was to share some experience on what it takes to make a RCM effort successful regardless of what methodology you or your business elect to apply.

In my quest to perfect a RCM methodology that focuses on manufacturing assets, I have come to understand that the most important thing to remember is this:

Make it your goal to learn the importance of each step of the process, follow the steps and stick to the process.

It is human nature to learn a process and to believe as soon as we understand that process, we can make it quicker, shorter, or faster. I can honestly say that I have always remained open to how we can improve the RCM Blitz™ process but each change must add value to the process or improve cycle time without compromising the outcome. Each year I have a client or facilitator come to me and ask to change the process, "Do we really need to write functions statements?" I always have the same answer, "If you are confident in your abilities and knowledge in RCM why are you asking me?" When I provide training, I begin the course by making the statement that each step of the process is in place for a specific reason, and that reason is to ensure the product of each RCM analysis. This process does not contain a single wasted step or exercise built to increase the facilitation cycle.

Does this mean the process can't be improved? Does it also mean that I have closed the book when it comes to change in the RCM process?

No, it just means I have become smarter in my old age! One of the greatest things that I have gained in creating this process is the number of RCM experts I now call friends. People like Jack Nicholas Jr., Derek Burley and Terry O'Hanlon. Anytime I consider making a change, I run the idea by my growing list of friends. Chances are my idea is not new and one of them has tried it out before.

While I may be a slow learner, I have never underestimated what I see as my strengths:

1. Leadership - Setting a vision, goals and direction. Plan-Act-Perform-Access-Repeat

2. Structure - Develop a process, continue to assess and improve using the leadership model.

3. Discipline - Stick to the process, let the experts answer the questions, implement the results, and perform the tasks.

One of the greatest values that come from facilitating, or participating in RCM, is the ability to understand the relationship between cause and effect. Those who participate in RCM gain the natural ability to become experts on Root Cause Analysis or Cause Mapping. This skill builds confidence in each individual involved in the process. They leave understanding that each failure can have multiple causes and different solutions. This understanding and skill, combined with RCM, and the results from having a complete maintenance strategy, creates a business environment where your workforce and products are now at a competitive advantage.

The Path Forward
While every book has an end, the story of RCM Blitz™ will continue to move forward. I look forward to future improvements in the process. Over the months it took to put my thoughts into this laptop, I have begun working with the Team at Allied Reliability to have RCM Blitz™ work together with a new tool AHM (Asset Health Matrix). Together RCM Blitz™, and AHM, will offer a complete maintenance strategy for critical assets and a comprehensive and efficient equipment maintenance plan (EMP) for the remaining balance of plant assets. The outcome of this effort will be the first complete, efficient, and affordable solution to a total plant maintenance strategy!

I also look forward to working with the Allied Reliability Team that includes some of the world's experts in reliability, including John Schultz, Chris Klosterman, Andy Page, Cary Repaz, Bill Keeter, and Chris Colson, to increase my knowledge in PdM tools, techniques and methods. I am thoroughly convinced that it is the human ability to continue to learn that keeps one young and alive.

In each phase of my career, I can point to individuals along the way who have made an impact on who I am as a person in business and in life. None have been more influential than my wife, Leslie Plucknette and my children. I look forward in the future to spending more time with those who inspire me, and with grandchildren on the way, home looks better than ever!

And lastly, I look forward to taking off the pounds that joined me at the rate of about half an ounce per analysis! My friend Mark Galley likes to compare equipment reliability to the human machine. About once a year we present together and because I am a slow learner I never seem to get out of the room before he starts making that comparison. I look forward to the time I get back to my pre-RCM body!

Thanks for taking the time to read and learn, it has made the time I took to record and share worthwhile!

Updates on the last three items

The Allied Reliability Team became the GPAllied Team in 2008 and in the past few years our team has developed tools and methods necessary to develop a complete maintenance and operations strategy to ensure reliability for an entire plant site or business enterprise. From developing equipment hierarchy to employing the most sophisticated tools and techniques our Asset Health Assurance process is bar none, best the world has to offer.

Life at home continues to be hectic but our family remains strong with love and support from all directions. With our first grandchild time at home is even more cherished as our home is filled with the toys and laughter of Iris Grace McCollister.

And finally the battle of the bulge continues – In 2009 I was able to shed 50 unneeded pounds and still today work on the discipline necessary to keep that weight off. Smaller meals, less carbs and steady daily exercise seem to be doing the trick!

DOUGLAS J. PLUCKNETTE

As the founder of RCM Blitz™ Doug has provided Reliability Centered Maintenance Training and services to numerous companies around the world.

Prior to his work as a consultant, Doug worked nineteen years at Eastman Kodak Company in Rochester, NY in positions as a skilled tradesperson, lead-person, maintenance supervisor, and reliability engineer. Doug holds a certificate in Reliability, Engineering and Maintenance from Rochester Institute of Technology.

Doug lives in Spencerport, New York with his wife and three children. In his spare time he enjoys hunting, fishing and golfing.

For the most up to date articles/information and discussion regarding RCM Blitz™ please visit my blog at www.rcmblitz.com. We have grown to about 700 visits a month over the past several years.

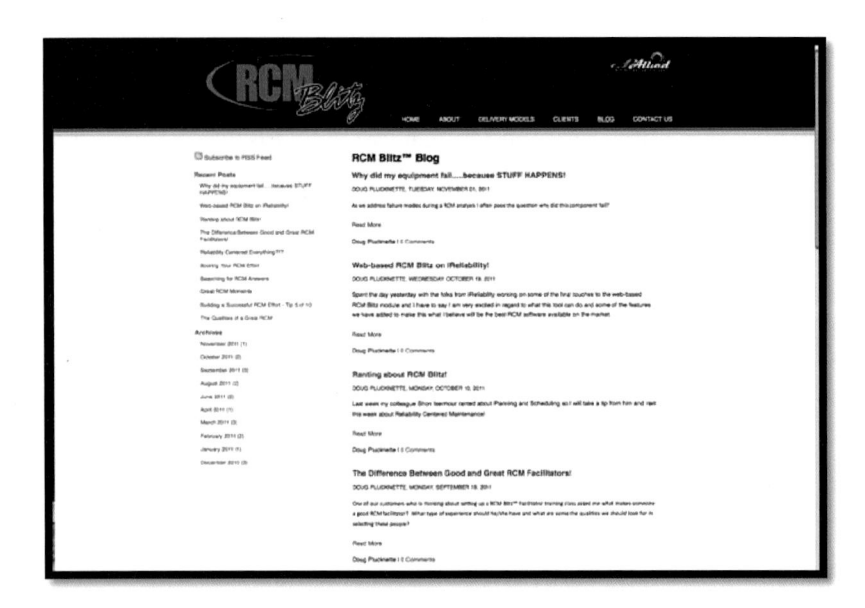

About Reliabilityweb.com

Created in 1999, Reliabilityweb.com provides educational information and peer-to-peer networking opportunities that enable safe and effective maintenance reliability and asset management for organizations around the world.

Activities Include:

Reliabilityweb.com® (www.reliabilityweb.com) includes educational articles, tips, video presentations, an industry event calendar and industry news. Updates are available through free email subscriptions and RSS feeds. **Confiabilidad.net** is a mirror site that is available in Spanish at www.confiabilidad.net

Uptime® Magazine (www.uptimemagazine.com) is a bi-monthly magazine launched in 2005 that is highly prized by the maintenance reliability and asset management community. Editions are obtainable in both print and digital.

Reliability Leadership Institute™ Conferences and Training Events

(www.maintenanceconference.com) offer events that range from unique, focused-training workshops and seminars to small focused conferences to large industry-wide events, including the International Maintenance Conference and The RELIABILITY Conference™.

MRO-Zone Bookstore (www.mro-zone.com) is an online bookstore offering a maintenance reliability and asset management focused library of books, DVDs and CDs published by Reliabilityweb.com.

Association of Asset Management Professionals

(www.maintenance.org) is a member organization and online community that encourages professional development and certification and supports information exchange and learning with 50,000+ members worldwide.

A Word About Social Good

Reliabilityweb.com is mission driven to deliver value and social good to the maintenance reliability and asset management communities. *Doing good work and making profit is not inconsistent*, and as a result of Reliabilityweb.com's mission-driven focus, financial stability and success has been the outcome. For over a decade, Reliabilityweb.com's positive contributions and commitment to the maintenance reliability and asset management communities have been unmatched.

Other Causes

Reliabilityweb.com has financially contributed to include industry associations, such as SMRP, AFE, STLE, ASME and ASTM, and community charities, including the Salvation Army, American Red Cross, Wounded Warrior Project, Paralyzed Veterans of America and the Autism Society of America. In addition, we are proud supporters of our U.S. Troops and first responders who protect our freedoms and way of life. That is only possible by being a for-profit company that pays taxes.

I hope you will get involved with and explore the many resources that are available to you through the Reliabilityweb.com network.

Warmest regards,
Terrence O'Hanlon
CEO, Reliabilityweb.com

Uptime® Elements™

A Reliability Framework and Asset Management System™

Technical Activities

REM — Reliability Engineering for Maintenance
- Ca — criticality analysis
- Rsd — reliability strategy development
- Cp — capital project management
- Re — reliability engineering
- Rca — root cause analysis
- Rcd — reliability centered design

ACM — Asset Condition Management
- Aci — asset condition information
- Vib — vibration analysis
- Fa — fluid analysis
- Ab — alignment and balancing
- Ut — ultrasound testing
- Ir — infrared thermal imaging
- Mt — motor testing
- Ndt — non destructive testing
- Lu — machinery lubrication

WEM — Work Execution Management
- Pm — preventive maintenance
- Ps — planning and scheduling
- De — defect elimination
- Odr — operator driven reliability
- Mro — mro-spares management
- Cmms — computerized maintenance management system

Leadership

LER — Leadership for Reliability
- Es — executive sponsorship
- Opx — operational excellence
- Hcm — human capital management
- Cbl — competency based learning
- Int — integrity
- Rj — reliability journey

Business Processes

AM — Asset Management
- Sp — strategy and plans
- Cr — corporate responsibility
- Samp — strategic asset management plan
- Dm — decision making
- Ri — risk management
- Ak — asset knowledge
- Alm — asset lifecycle management
- Pi — performance indicators
- Ci — continuous improvement

Reliabilityweb.com's Asset Management Timeline

Business Needs Analysis → Design → Create/Acquire → Operate / Maintain / Modify/Upgrade → Dispose/Renew → Residual Liabilities

Asset Lifecycle

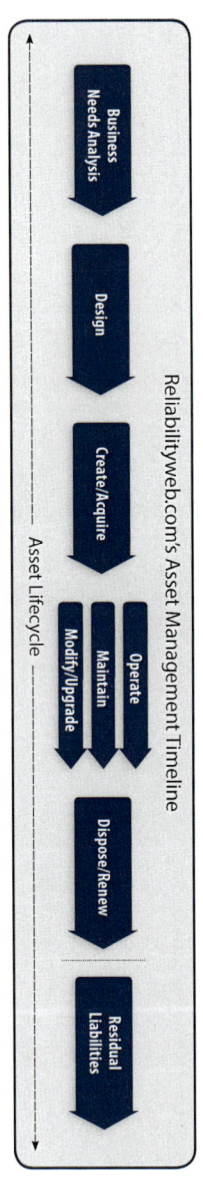

Reprinted with permission from NetexpressUSA Inc. d/b/a Reliabilityweb.com and its affiliates. Copyright © 2016-2017. All rights reserved. No part of this graphic may be reproduced or transmitted in any form or by any means without the prior express written consent of NetexpressUSA Inc. Reliabilityweb.com®, Uptime® Elements™ and A Reliability Framework and Asset Management System™ are trademarks and registered trademarks of NetexpressUSA Inc. in the U.S. and several other countries.

reliabilityweb.com • maintenance.org • reliabilityleadership.com

Reliabilityweb.com® and Uptime® Magazine Mission: **To make the people we serve safer and more successful.** One way we support this mission is to suggest a reliability system for asset performance management as pictured above. Our use of the Uptime Elements is designed to assist you in categorizing and organizing your own Body of Knowledge (BoK) whether it be through training, articles, books or webinars. Our hope is to make YOU safer and more successful.